Working Together to Improve Literacy

How to set goals, implement, and assess school-wide reading and writing initiatives

GRAHAM FOSTER

Pembroke Publishers Limited

© 2008 Pembroke Publishers
538 Hood Road
Markham, Ontario, Canada L3R 3K9
www.pembrokepublishers.com

Distributed in the U.S. by Stenhouse Publishers
477 Congress Street
Portland, ME 04101
www.stenhouse.com

We acknowledge the financial support of the Government of Canada through the Book Publishing Industry Development Program (BPIDP) for our publishing activities.

We acknowledge the Government of Ontario through the Ontario Media Development Corporation's Ontario Book Initiative.

Library and Archives Canada Cataloguing in Publication

Foster, Graham
   Working together to improve literacy : how to set goals, implement and assess school-wide reading and writing initiatives / Graham Foster.

Includes index.
ISBN 978-1-55138-224-1

   1. Reading (Secondary)—Ontario. 2. Language arts (Secondary)—Ontario. I. Title.

LC149.F68 2008   428.4'09713   C2008-903364-7

Editor: Jane McNulty
Cover Design: John Zehethofer
Typesetting: Jay Tee Graphics Ltd.

Printed and bound in Canada
9 8 7 6 5 4 3 2 1

Contents

1

Collaborative Instructional Practice

Establishing Fundamental Principles

Over the past several years, educators in many jurisdictions have participated enthusiastically in school-based professional development to improve literacy programs. Typically, these professional development initiatives aim to coordinate instructional practice across grades and content areas. Why have so many schools dedicated financial and human resources to coordinating literacy instruction? Why do teachers, literacy coaches, and administrators spend time and energy analyzing what distinguishes successful from less successful collaborative literacy programs? This book explores answers to these and other fundamental questions.

Two main motivators underlie collaborative literacy programs. By working together to enhance their school's literacy instruction and by ensuring best practice in program coordination, teachers enjoy professional affirmation. At the same time, they enhance their students' language learning and their school's overall success.

Working together to achieve a school-wide collaborative literacy goal means that administrators, literacy coaches, and teachers:

- agree to coordinate instruction focused on one or two important literacy goals
- select the goal or goals in a process that involves honest, respectful discussion about student needs
- identify and implement key instructional strategies and use the same vocabulary to describe these strategies to enhance student achievement across grades and subjects
- meet regularly to discuss, learn about, refine, and assess their implementation of instructional strategies related to the targeted literacy goal(s)

By its very nature, school-wide coordination of literacy programs requires collaboration. Colleagues must work together in order to set priorities, share ideas, and assess the benefits of the instructional strategies they have chosen. They meet regularly to discuss, select, and track shared goals and approaches. They collaborate to plan professional development activities and to determine how to assess student achievement. A spirit of collaboration encourages colleagues to express their concerns and frustrations freely with each other as they exchange feedback about their implementation efforts.

Collaborative literacy projects are more successful in some schools than in others. Why is this the case? The disparities reflect differences in school leadership, in availability of resources, and in the level of respect for collaborative processes. Attempts at coordinating instructional practice will flounder unless administrators and other school leaders become active, even passionate, participants. Some projects fail because inadequate time and resources have been allocated. In contrast, schools with a burning desire to launch a viable collaborative literacy project manage to find the time, the money, and the people. They carefully review and emulate processes followed by schools that have experienced success. (Later chapters will consider these topics in greater depth.)

What Are the Benefits of Coordinating Literacy Instruction?

Schools have two important reasons for coordinating literacy instruction: students benefit and educators benefit. Professional literature on the topic of best practice and effective schools—for example, Michael Fullan's *Breakthrough* (2006)—argues convincingly that collaborative, coordinated instruction clearly enhances student achievement.

In my former role as a language arts supervisor and in my current role as a private literacy consultant, I have observed that teachers often use varying terminology to describe approaches to teaching and learning. If you were to challenge teachers to identify differences between "skills" and "strategies," for example, you would probably note discrepancies in the use of these terms. I have witnessed countless improvements in student achievement when educators in a school work together to devise a shared terminology related to learning tasks. For instance, if educators have forged a shared understanding of terminology across grades and content areas, they consistently use the term "skills" to describe *what* students are challenged to do. They use the term "strategies" to describe *how* students will do something.

Similarly, I have seen teachers expand their shared understanding of strategies by using consistent vocabulary when they challenge students to identify:

- how they will proceed before they begin work on a learning task; in other words, how they will plan their approach to the task
- how they will proceed during work on the task (this is especially relevant for struggling students)
- how they will conclude a learning task; in other words, how they will polish or refine their work

No matter what the grade or subject, research has shown that when teachers work from a shared model such as the one described above, using identical vocabulary, both they and their students benefit. Their shared understandings enhance communication and help students transfer their learning from one content area to another. When a school-wide literacy project based on collaboration is running smoothly, transitions between grades and between subject areas become smoother for students as well.

To help ensure a successful collaborative literacy project, teachers adopt the same language to describe strategies students can use before, during, and after reading an unfamiliar text, writing a first draft, or tackling any other language learning task. Teachers' consistent use of terminology related to a shared instructional model clearly supports students' learning. Also, coherent communication with family members and with the community beyond the school results from use of similar language to describe shared goals and shared plans.

When asked why they favor working together to coordinate practice, educators typically reply that they gain great professional satisfaction from the collaborative process. Teachers spend most of their time working with students rather than with colleagues. Professional dialogue and interaction with peers offer a refreshing change of pace. More importantly, when teachers see that collaboration and coordinated practice really do boost student achievement, their enthusiasm sustains their commitment to the school's literacy project. Literature about effective organizations, including effective schools, argues that working hard is not enough to improve instruction. The key to improved instruction and improved student learning lies in teachers working together to implement a shared repertoire of research-supported instructional strategies. To learn more about this topic, refer to *The Fifth Discipline: The Art and Practice of the Learning Organization* by Peter M. Senge (2006), and *Teamwork: Setting the Standard for Collaborative Teaching, Grades 5-9*, by Monique D. Wild, Amanda S. Mayeux, and Kathryn P. Edmonds (2008).

While this book occasionally cites relevant professional literature, its contents are based primarily on my personal observations of several school-based collaborative literacy projects over many years. In my experience as language arts supervisor and more recently as a private consultant, I have observed that some school-based collaborative literacy projects work very well and generate a great deal of enthusiasm within the school community. Others yield limited success and little satisfaction for participants. This book presents principles and strategies for success. These principles and strategies have emerged from extensive observation of school-wide literacy projects along with the professional development that supports these initiatives.

Ensuring Success

The references in this book to "collaborative literacy projects" rather than to "collaborative language arts projects" are deliberate. Today, many schools recognize that students' literacy is best developed across all content areas. These schools have adopted a cross-curricular focus on literacy. Program or curriculum documents in many jurisdictions highlight the importance of shared responsibility for literacy instruction across all subject disciplines. When teachers emphasize reading and writing skills in all content areas, they achieve a double benefit. Not only do children's reading and writing abilities improve, but students also achieve better results in subjects other than language arts. Dedicated teachers recognize that language proficiency is the foundation for student learning across all grades and subject areas.

My experience working with schools has shown me that, to ensure success, administrators and literacy coaches must demonstrate firm commitment to the following six fundamental principles:

- Respecting collaborative decisions and valuing inquiry
- Defining the role of the literacy coach or literacy team members
- Securing the principal's commitment
- Separating personal from collegial professional development
- Planning for the highest level of professional development
- Emphasizing legal program requirements

The key to improved instruction and improved student learning lies in teachers working together to implement a shared repertoire of research-supported instructional strategies.

Dedicated teachers recognize that language proficiency is the foundation for student learning across all grades and subject areas.

Before a school launches a collaborative literacy project, coaches and administrators should clearly explain and then discuss the six principles above with all participants. Throughout the project, effective leaders consistently demonstrate their unflagging commitment to these fundamental principles, which are elaborated below.

Respecting Collaborative Decisions and Valuing Inquiry

Coordinated instructional practice cannot be dictated to teachers from "on high." To be effective, coordinated practice must accommodate the active collegial involvement of teachers and other stakeholders in key aspects of planning and implementation:

- Goal setting
- Developing a professional development plan
- Discussing and implementing instructional strategies
- Assessing and celebrating progress

> Effective plans for coordinated practice emphasize that teachers are also learners, problem solvers, and professionals committed to the refinement of practice.

Effective plans for coordinated practice emphasize that teachers are also learners, problem solvers, and professionals committed to the refinement of practice. Researchers such as Marilyn Duncan in *Literacy Coaching* (2006) have described this emphasis as an "inquiry approach" to instruction and program coordination.

Collegial professional development hinges on the dedication of time and resources for planning, learning, implementing, and assessing. Many schools build collegial professional development time into their schedules and budget for release time and purchase of learning resources for both teachers and students.

From the outset, school administrators and literacy coaches must display their commitment to collaborative decision making related to coordinated practice. They do so by actions as well as by words. They create conditions conducive to genuine involvement of all stakeholders in decision making. They encourage all teachers to participate in goal setting and they demonstrate respect for everyone who works in the school. They invite ongoing feedback about the program coordination process and they welcome suggestions for improvement.

Nothing thwarts program coordination more than treating teachers as technicians rather than as professionals. Anyone who imposes programs to be followed rather than encouraging collaborative decision making views teachers as technicians. Often this attitude manifests itself as a decision to implement a pre-packaged program. In *Teaching: The Universe of Discourse* (1968), James Moffett warned about the dangers of "program panaceas":

> We build the right facilities, organize the best courses of study, work out the finest methods, create the appropriate materials, and then, come September, the wrong students walk through the door. (p. 13)

Collegial coordination of instruction views the teacher as the most important resource in improving students' learning. Teachers are a much more valuable resource than any print resource or pre-packaged program. Teachers possess flexibility and insight. They recognize that learning materials and approaches that work well with some students might fail with others. A teacher's personal learning complemented by collegial professional development and coordinated practice represents the most surefire way to enhance students' learning. (Chapter 3 elaborates on the topic of collegial professional development.)

Administrators and literacy coaches should take every opportunity to highlight the two main reasons for collegial professional development:

- Student learning is enhanced when teachers coordinate selected aspects of instruction.
- Teachers derive immense professional satisfaction from collaborative projects.

In his highly influential book *Breakthrough* (2006), Michael Fullan points out that while collegial professional development initiatives sometimes encounter bumps along the way, enhanced professionalism and documented benefits to student learning tend to sustain projects over time. The link between coordinated practice and improved student achievement has long been noted by Fullan and by other researchers who have studied effective schools. For example, in *Teacher Leadership* (2000), Ann Lieberman and Lynne Miller stress how professional community building and active involvement in planning, implementing, and assessing key instructional strategies benefit teachers as well as students. An enhanced sense of professionalism and confidence sustains teachers, especially during the rough patches that inevitably occur during program coordination efforts.

Administrators and literacy coaches wisely voice the fact that even though teachers employ diverse instructional approaches, they can still collaborate on key aspects of instruction. Some teachers are relatively structured in their teaching styles; others are less structured. Teachers' interests and strengths vary. Collegial program coordination does not mean that teachers abandon successful aspects of their own personal instructional styles. Successful program coordination ensures that one or two key goals can be accomplished by means of diverse teaching styles. Administrators and literacy coaches recognize that individuals will not sabotage something if they feel themselves to be a vital part of it. If administrators and coaches devote time and energy to facilitate collegial decision making on the part of all participants, they effectively set the stage for successful program coordination.

> The link between coordinated practice and improved student achievement has long been noted by Fullan and by other researchers who have studied effective schools.

Defining the Role of the Literacy Coach

Schools committed to coordinated instructional practice often assign individuals to leadership roles with titles such as "literacy program coordinator," "language arts program coordinating teacher," or "literacy coach." ("Literacy coach" is the term used in this book.) Alternatively, schools sometimes appoint a literacy leadership team. Teachers appointed to language arts or literacy leadership positions must possess the attributes listed on the following page.

- Deep knowledge of the legally prescribed English Language Arts curriculum as well as other legally prescribed curricula related to a school's literacy project
- Recognized success as a language arts or literacy teacher
- Extensive current professional development work related to language arts and literacy
- Genuine commitment to collaborative program coordination and related professional development
- Genuine commitment to an inquiry approach to professional development in which individuals and groups:
  - pose questions, learn together, and demonstrate their learning in the classroom
  - select appropriate instructional strategies
  - assess the impact of those strategies
  - refine their practice
  - publish results
- Strong organizational and communication skills
- Respectful, encouraging attitude toward colleagues

Sometimes schools establish literacy leadership teams to promote best practice in the school. In such a case, team members must demonstrate the same attributes as for a literacy coach. No matter what type of leadership structure exists to support literacy learning in a school, the goal of building capacity—that is, helping teachers work confidently together to coordinate instructional practice in their school—should be front and centre. Rosemarye Taylor's and Valerie Doyle Collins' *Literacy Leadership for Grades 5-12* (2003) is one of several excellent resources that discuss this important principle.

The Literacy Coach's Responsibilities

Teachers who accept literacy leadership roles should clearly explain how they perceive their role and their responsibilities both to colleagues and to the community beyond the school. They can clarify their responsibilities in meetings with colleagues, in conferences with family members, and in the school newsletter. Usually, a literacy leadership position does not involve performance appraisal of teachers. Therefore, literacy coaches can capitalize on the fact that they are facilitators rather than evaluators of teacher performance. Typically, a literacy coach's role focuses on matters such as:

- Advising colleagues about legal program requirements
- Serving as an on-site consultant regarding methodology and resources
- Ordering professional resources
- Planning activities to involve parents and guardians in promoting children's literacy and supporting school programs
- Interpreting the school district's funding guidelines and protocol for school-based professional development
- Completing documentation required by the district for school-based professional development initiatives
- Organizing collegial professional development related to coordinated practice goals

- Meeting with other literacy coaches and literacy leaders within and beyond the school district

Jennifer Allen's *Becoming a Literacy Leader* (2006) elaborates on the roles and responsibilities of literacy coaches and other literacy leaders serving a school. To be trusted and effective while fulfilling their role, literacy coaches must remain consistently attentive and sensitive to each colleague's questions and challenges. Instead of rushing in with advice, they make a habit of listening first. When invited to work with students in a colleague's classroom, coaches identify students' needs and interests as touchstones for any instructional suggestions they offer. Coaches who are able to "show" as well as "tell" represent a priceless asset to a school community. If literacy leaders are willing to model instructional approaches with students, they establish their credibility with teachers. They enhance their credibility further when they encourage colleagues to model instructional approaches that are pivotal to a school's collaborative literacy project. Effective literacy coaches happily share the stage with their peers.

Moreover, effective literacy coaches aspire to the highest professional standards in carrying out their responsibilities. While encouraging honesty and risk-taking on the part of their colleagues, they respect confidences and openly admit that they too have questions, doubts, and concerns about the school's literacy program. They enthusiastically acknowledge the contributions of others and seek regular opportunities to offer genuine compliments. If and when they hear negative comments about the school's literacy project, they invite critics to suggest refinements or improvements. They avoid negative or judgmental comments about colleagues—even those who could be described as "test-your-patience" personality types. While encouraging colleagues to learn together, they model their own learning aimed at improving coordinated instructional practice.

More that anything else, literacy coaches promote ongoing dialogue among colleagues about best practice, current school realities, and possible ways to enhance instruction. In *Literacy Coaching* (2006), Marilyn Duncan argues that such ongoing professional conversations are fundamental to improving a school's literacy program.

While working within their clearly defined leadership roles, literacy coaches must also establish a close working relationship with principals and other administrators. Together, they develop and articulate plans to achieve successful program coordination within the school. By clearly outlining a specific role description for a literacy coach in staff handbooks and in school publications, administrators underscore the vital importance of this role.

Securing the Principal's Commitment

Successful collaborative literacy projects always rely on the active, collegial involvement of school-based administrators, especially the principal or vice-principal. Projects suffer when school administrators avoid involvement because they feel they are simply too busy. If administrators sidestep involvement, they send a message to their colleagues that they consider collegial program coordination irrelevant to the success of the school.

The Principal's Role

Ideally, principals or vice-principals take every opportunity to express their personal conviction that collaborative, coordinated instruction benefits all children served by the school. More specifically, principals should assume the following responsibilities:

- Clearly articulate their own assessment of the school's literacy program strengths and needs while inviting colleagues to do the same
- Introduce the topic of collaborative program coordination when they interview prospective teachers who have applied for jobs at the school
- Make clear to their staff and colleagues that adequate finances, human resources, and time will be dedicated to collaborative program coordination
- State clearly that they intend to participate actively in collegial professional development and follow through with their intentions
- Demonstrate support for literacy coaches
- Emphasize that collegiality will be honoured in the development and implementation of collaborative plans
- Emphasize openness about goals and professional development while conveying a clear message that passivity is not an option
- Encourage open communication among participants and put strategies in place to deal with disagreements and frustrations
- Help develop and articulate shared understandings about research that reinforces the link between coordinated practice and effective literacy learning
- Offer ongoing feedback to teachers about implementation of instructional practice related to program coordination goals

Professional literature highlights a principal's fundamental leadership role in maximizing a school's overall student achievement.

Professional literature highlights a principal's fundamental leadership role in maximizing a school's overall student achievement. In *School Leadership That Works* (2005), Robert L. Marzano summarizes the research on this topic. For a practical guide to the principal's role in literacy leadership, David Booth's *The Literacy Principal* (2007) is highly recommended. These books elaborate on the principal's role in creating a literacy culture within the school, in sharing ideas about research-supported literacy practice, and in actively participating in and supporting collaborative literacy projects.

Separating Collegial From Personal Professional Development

No matter what plan for coordinated practice emerges in a school, literacy coaches should make a clear distinction as early as possible between two critical dimensions of professional development—the collegial and the personal.

Collaborative instructional programs typically go hand in hand with collegial professional development. Educators plan professional development for all colleagues based on the one or two collaborative goals that the staff has chosen. The plan does not necessarily entail that all teachers will engage in identical professional development activities related to the chosen goal(s). Sub-groups and individuals are free to choose different professional development activities. In many cases, on the other hand, colleagues may decide that professional development activities for the entire group are appropriate. The key point is that teachers commit to regular meetings to share their learning as they refine their coordinated instructional practice.

Personal Professional Development

Because of obvious differences in qualifications and teaching experience, individual teachers have individual professional development needs. Beginning teachers working outside their area of expertise will make different personal professional development choices compared to more experienced teachers who are well versed in a particular program. Novice teachers will probably choose different convention sessions, workshops, sharing sessions, articles, books, professional development videos, and mentorship plans compared to their more seasoned peers. Also, many jurisdictions emphasize individual teachers' learning priorities in performance assessment interviews. In consultation with their principal, teachers choose a personal learning path that is tailored for them, apply their learning in the classroom, and assess results.

Literacy coaches can serve as valuable resources for teachers as they plan their personal professional development. Effective coaches nurture an inquiry approach to professional learning while sharing their instructional expertise with teachers one on one. They invite individual teachers to reflect on their concerns about literacy instruction in their classrooms and to discover resources that might help them address these concerns. Coaches help teachers implement instructional strategies and assess the benefit of these strategies, thus providing a valuable service in the spirit of inquiry learning. In supporting teachers' pursuit of individual professional development, literacy coaches play the role of active, respectful listeners. They help colleagues assess their needs, analyze their strengths, and set their own priorities.

Effective coaches nurture an inquiry approach to professional learning while sharing their instructional expertise with teachers one on one.

Collegial Professional Development

Collegial professional development emphasizes shared learning focused on coordination of key aspects of instruction. Following regularly scheduled discussions of program strengths and student needs, teachers reach consensus on the goal(s) and instructional strategies to which they will devote their energies. The collegial professional development tied to these goals and instructional strategies employs the same inquiry approach as that followed in the pursuit of individual professional development. Teachers ask each other many questions and strive to find answers to refine instructional practice. They apply their learning in classroom settings, share observations with colleagues, and then try out further refinements in an ongoing cycle. (See the diagram on the following page.)

While collegial professional development may include listening to guest speakers and discussing journal articles, it also expands these notions of professional development to include collaborative planning for:

- Instruction
- Collegial goal setting
- Selection and implementation of instructional strategies
- Assessment of results

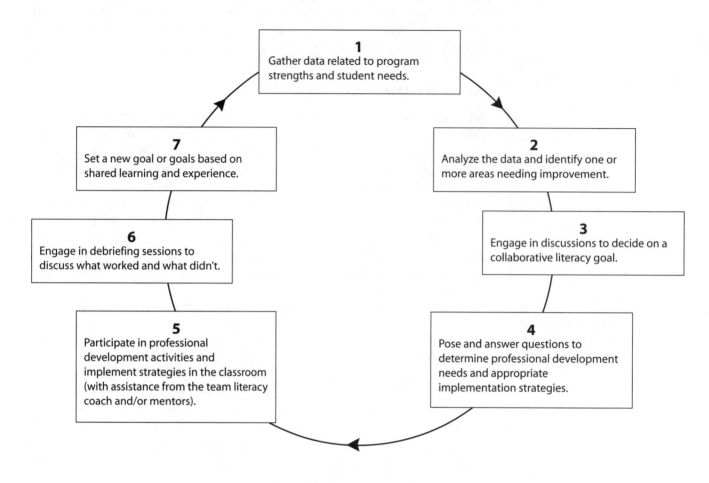

Collegial professional development often involves mentorship, peer partnerships, group development of instructional resources and assessment tools, and, finally, group assessment activities such as marking student writing samples together. Mentorship typically takes the form of an experienced teacher meeting regularly with a less experienced teacher to share materials, answer questions, and provide observational feedback about lessons. Partnership often takes the form of teachers working in small groups to develop and share instructional materials.

I have witnessed two successful forms of collegial professional development tied to program coordination:

- The entire school staff identifies a goal or a limited number of goals geared to program coordination and negotiates a common plan related to the selected goal(s).
- The entire staff identifies a goal or a limited number of goals for program coordination and—following the ever-present guideline that all teachers will participate—organizes sub-groups that develop diverse implementation plans that are still essentially connected to the overall goal(s).

Professional Development in Action

An example of the second option described above occurred in a Kindergarten to Grade 6 school whose literacy goal centred on revision of students' writing across grades and content areas according to specific criteria. Colleagues agreed that for Grades 4 to 6 students, teachers would not evaluate final draft writing until they had gathered evidence that students had revised their writing according to specific criteria. These criteria included:

- My word choice is precise and colorful.
- My sentences are varied in their construction.
- My story presents and resolves the central character's conflict.
- I have correctly capitalized proper nouns.

Teachers agreed that Grades 4 to 6 students would use sticky notes or highlighters to indicate where and how their compositions met selected criteria. Students wrote each criterion on a separate sticky note and drew lines in pencil pointing to evidence of the criteria in their written work. Using different colored highlighters, students marked particular words and sentences in their compositions. They drew attention to narrative elements such as conflict and climax, and noted grammatical conventions such as capitalization of proper nouns. Marking up their writing reinforced their attentiveness to the criteria and enabled them to share strategies and compare notes with classmates.

Primary teachers in the school, on the other hand, pointed out that the writing process is typically slower for younger students. As a result, primary teachers opted to be more casual in their implementation of the revision strategy. Through modeling, they showed their students how to check one's writing to ensure that it meets specific criteria. However, these primary teachers avoided becoming rule-bound and refrained from insisting that students *always* demonstrate revision in their writing to align with specific criteria.

In secondary grades, teachers often employ a sub-group approach to a common goal. Teachers break into subject-area teams to plan instructional strategies related to a shared goal. For instance, one school's science, mathematics, and language arts teachers agreed to emphasize reading comprehension strategies in the context of their respective subject areas on an ongoing basis. The sub-groups met to plan instructional strategies related to this shared goal. Occasionally they met as a larger group to solicit advice from each other and to compare notes.

Despite the variations in emphasis, this school's teachers feel secure knowing they are pursuing a common goal established in a spirit of collaboration and collegiality. They look forward to meeting regularly as a team to discuss implementation strategies, to share suggestions for refinements, and to plan appropriate assessment.

Emphasizing Legal Program Requirements

Coordination of instructional practice is best served when school leaders stress the importance of legal program requirements. Leaders are wise to establish clearly and early that collegial professional development activities must be directly connected to legal program requirements. In most jurisdictions, teachers do not spearhead curriculum development. Rather, they are contracted to teach externally set programs of study. Teachers can provide feedback on curriculum documents as the documents are in development and they can serve on review committees. However, once the curriculum has been validated and approved, teachers have a legal obligation to implement it.

Literacy coaches and school administrators often point to legal program requirements as the gold reserve behind the currency of school coordination projects. Program coordination leads to improved student success in achieving the prescribed learning outcomes.

Occasionally, teachers who have learned about an innovative instructional approach at a conference or in a university course become passionate about its adoption in their school. While literacy coaches and school administrators always welcome suggestions for improved coordinated practice, they must also challenge enthusiastic teachers to link new instructional strategies to the legal program mandates. If teachers believe that the legally mandated program is out-of-date or imperfect, they should voice concerns and present specific suggestions to those responsible for the program's development and adoption. They may do so through individual correspondence with educational authorities. Another route is through group submissions developed and forwarded by school districts, or by organizations such as the International Reading Association.

In addition, literacy coaches should ensure that all teachers are provided with copies of legal program documents. In my experience, teachers sometimes do not own copies of curriculum documents, whether outdated or current. Coaches should also ensure that all complementary curriculum support documents published by the state, by the provincial Department of Education, or by their school district are widely available in the school. This type of support material often deals with important topics such as methodology, text resources, assessment, and differentiated instruction. Because these documents furnish guidance related to the legal program of studies, they should be freely available to teachers in places such as the school resource centre, the principal's office, and the school staffroom.

Furthermore, literacy coaches should check to see whether prescribed or currently recommended student learning resources for legal programs are in stock and in use in the school. Again, in my experience, teachers often use out-of-date or unauthorized resources as core student texts. When such is the case, literacy coaches and administrators must strive to provide and promote currently authorized resources. If some teachers cling to out-of-date resources in resistance to curriculum change, the principal must clearly articulate the school's obligations to implement the legally prescribed curriculum.

This book will describe a specific process for collegial engagement in goal setting, implementation, and assessment geared to collaborative literacy instruction. The chapters that follow offer suggestions for highly effective professional development. The book concludes with descriptions of specific collaborative projects related to best practice in reading and writing.

While literacy coaches and school administrators always welcome suggestions for improved coordinated practice, they must also challenge enthusiastic teachers to link new instructional strategies to the legal program mandates.

Checklist for Literacy Coaches and Administrators

Literacy coaches and administrators may use this checklist to ensure they have met the following criteria in developing and implementing specific plans for coordinated instructional practice:

☐ We have clearly articulated the benefits of coordinated instructional practice in our school: enhanced student achievement and enhanced professional satisfaction for educators.

☐ We have consistently demonstrated our commitment to coordinated instructional practice in our school and to our specific roles in facilitating collaboration.

☐ We have dedicated adequate time and financial resources to our school's collaborative literacy project.

☐ We have published specific role definitions for literacy coaches or literacy team members.

☐ We have articulated the principal's role in championing collegial professional development.

☐ We have clearly described our sense of how collegial professional development complements personal professional development.

☐ We have ensured that teachers possess current copies of prescribed legal program documents as well as complementary resources published by our local educational authorities.

☐ We have emphasized our commitment to a collaborative literacy project related to legally mandated programs of study that will benefit all children served by our school.

2

Goal Setting

Reviewing the Process for Collaborative Coordination

To plan a viable collaborative literacy project, administrators and literacy coaches must stop to ask themselves, "Where do we begin?" The first step is to amplify the rationale for literacy program coordination that colleagues have developed (as described in Chapter 1) with a clearly articulated implementation plan. The implementation plan should outline the following:

- Goal-setting activities
- Suggestions for professional development
- Implementation strategies and timeframes
- Regular meeting times to share materials, observations, and concerns
- Data-gathering methods related to assessing the project's benefits to students
- Ways to publicize and celebrate the project within and beyond the school community

School district or external funding guidelines may mean that decisions related to some of these items are non-negotiable. If so, literacy coaches must share as much information with colleagues as possible about mandated stipulations related to funding the school's collaborative literacy project.

Throughout a project's implementation phase, effective administrators and literacy coaches extend an open invitation to all stakeholders to offer suggestions for ways to support the project. To promote the project further, leaders should clarify which print, media, and human resources, as well as release time allotments, will be available to participants. Ideally, ample release time for professional development and team meetings will be part of the plan. Release time signals that the project is not just an add-on to a busy school day but is, rather, an integral part of overall program implementation.

Setting Clear and Attainable Goals

Early in the planning phase of a project, literacy coaches help guide colleagues toward setting clear and attainable goals. Participants must recognize that they need to establish priorities—they can realistically select no more than one or two specific collaborative literacy goals. Every day, teachers face overwhelming curriculum demands as well as tightened requirements for documentation of individual program plans for students with special needs or for students in modified programs. If teachers try to coordinate a long list of literacy goals while coping with these pressures, they might as well aim for none. Many viable projects, quite wisely, focus on a single goal.

Keep in mind that the one or two collaborative goals eventually chosen should be reasonably specific. For instance, goals such as "Improving Students' Reading Abilities" or "Improving Students' Writing" are too general. Projects require a comparatively narrow focus, for example, "Coordinating Reading Comprehension Strategies Across All Grades and Content Areas" or "Effective Revision of Writing Across All Grades and Content Areas."

In my work as a consultant, I have seen colleagues fail to develop a shared implementation plan because their goal was too general. For instance, if a project's goal is "Improving Students' Reading," some teachers may interpret the goal to mean improving reading comprehension strategies. Others could interpret the goal to mean improving higher-level thinking skills. Still others might interpret the goal to mean increasing the amount of independent reading completed by students. Leaders should explain that in selecting one or two clearly focused priorities for program coordination, teachers are still free to set different priorities for their own professional development. Collaborating with colleagues to achieve a highly focused project goal never implies the sacrifice of personal goals for professional development.

Besides focusing on too many goals or on goals that are too general, two other factors can jeopardize a collaborative literacy project. Both the constant switching of goals and the demoralizing effect of naysayers can throw a project off course. In my capacity as consultant, I have twice walked away from projects in which teachers identified a collaborative goal and then changed it from meeting to meeting. Weeks passed without any concrete planning for implementation of a shared goal. Again, colleagues must bear in mind that the selection of one or two priorities for program coordination in a school year is not a life sentence. Colleagues can and usually should select a different goal the following year. Principals and literacy coaches must sometimes stress that timeframe guidelines are important in setting goals. These guidelines must be respected. Different priorities can be established in subsequent school years.

Responding to Naysayers

Naysayers are colleagues who persistently point out perceived flaws or weaknesses in their school's collaborative literacy plan. Effective leaders remain calm and diplomatic when responding to expressions of dissent. In truth, critics often voice valid concerns about particular aspects of a project.

The most productive initial response to criticism is for coaches to reinforce that suggestions for improvement are always welcome. However, they should then qualify that reassurance by stating that pointing out flaws but doing nothing to help eradicate them is unacceptable. Once again, coaches' reminders about the desirability of separating collegial and personal professional development are helpful. Educators willing to make compromises for the sake of achieving a shared goal can still opt to pursue individual goals to enrich their own professional lives.

Four Options for Goal Setting

The goal-setting process can begin in one of four ways:

1. Focused discussion about goal setting
2. A best-practice overview followed by focused discussion about goal setting
3. Individual reading of selected best-practice texts followed by focused discussion about goal setting
4. A collegial program assessment process followed by focused discussion about goal setting

Each of these options will be discussed below. For all four options, colleagues must take the preliminary step of reviewing relevant data, such as:

- Student referral information, including information about the numbers of special needs students served by the school and the types of services offered
- Numbers of students in modified programs
- Survey information gathered from students and their family members
- Assessment data gathered from previous school projects
- Report card data
- Standardized test data

The key question to explore at this stage is: "What do these data tell us about potential goals and priorities for program coordination in our school?"

Option 1: Focused Discussion About Goal Setting

Goal setting often begins with focused collegial discussion about current strengths and needs in the school's literacy program based on the kinds of data listed above. Typically, the principal and/or literacy coach presents the data at a goal-setting meeting. After the presentation, colleagues discuss goal setting and planning. Participants jot notes as they discuss answers to key questions such as the following (the list of questions can be displayed on chart paper or photocopied and distributed):

- What are the strengths in our current language arts/literacy program?
- What student learning needs would benefit most from coordinated practice?
- What do you see as our top priority for coordinated instruction?
- What kinds of professional development do we need to organize?
- What instructional strategies will we emphasize?
- How often will we meet to discuss plans, concerns, and results?
- How can we assess students' progress vis-à-vis our shared goal(s)?
- What are the roles and responsibilities of each member of our team?

Questions such as these help guide participants toward selecting and refining collaborative literacy projects that are clearly related to the school's current reality and to specific plans to improve that reality. The link between thorough and honest discussion and the development of specific improvement plans has been

The link between thorough and honest discussion and the development of specific improvement plans has been emphasized widely in professional literature.

emphasized widely in professional literature. Examples include *Leading Beyond the Walls* by Frances Hesselbein et al. (1999), *Teacher Leadership* by Ann Lieberman and Lynne Miller (2000), and *School Leadership That Works* by Robert J. Marzano et al. (2005). (Refer to the List of Works Consulted at the back of this book.)

Note that whichever option colleagues choose to begin the goal-setting process, they can employ a Think-Pair-Share strategy as the next step in goal setting. After a period of individual reflection (Think), participants talk to a partner (Pair), and then present their ideas to the larger group (Share).

Option 2: Best-Practice Overview Followed by Focused Discussion

Chapter 3 in this book advises that listening to a guest speaker should never be a school's only professional development option. However, colleagues sometimes decide that a best-practice overview might help them select and refine a collaborative literacy goal. An overview session on topics such as "Best Practice in Reading" or "Possibilities for Differentiated Literacy Instruction" helps teachers affirm effective practice already in place in their school. At the same time, they explore possibilities for program improvement and narrow their focus for coordination. In my experience, best-practice overviews that present a range of practical instructional suggestions often succeed in helping educators set priorities for coordination as well as for their own professional development.

The adage about prophets being shunned in their own country often applies to introductory best-practice overviews. Therefore, it is common for literacy coaches to propose the names of outside experts to present the overview. During preliminary discussions about the presentation, teachers are sometimes invited to recommend possible presenters. To locate presenters who possess the requisite expertise and credibility, literacy coaches sometimes consult with district central office personnel. Alternatively, they can contact local branches of professional organizations such as the International Reading Association.

An external speaker can inform teachers about collaborative goals and strategies implemented by other schools. The speaker's far-ranging perspective sends a powerful message that the school is not working in isolation in its commitment to collaborative literacy instruction. Most importantly, an outside expert often reinforces that as colleagues spend time reflecting on priorities, they can also celebrate the excellent research-supported instructional practices already in place in their school.

Following a best-practice overview session, literacy coaches usually engage colleagues in a brief follow-up discussion about program strengths already evident in the school, along with possibilities for program coordination suggested by the presenter. Teachers' confidence and morale are boosted if the best-practice overview they attend confirms that they are "on the right track." I believe that such validation is vitally important for teachers as they confront the daily stresses and challenges of teaching. School leaders wisely offer as much genuine affirmation as possible. An outside expert, however, can lend a great deal of additional reassurance and reinforcement. In the debriefing session after the presentation, literacy coaches should stress that collaboration focuses on "what we do together" and not necessarily on "what is new." One key question to explore at this point is: What has the speaker suggested that we might realistically do together?

An external speaker can inform teachers about collaborative goals and strategies implemented by other schools. The speaker's far-ranging perspective sends a powerful message that the school is not working in isolation in its commitment to collaborative literacy instruction.

Option 3: Individual Reading of Texts Followed by Focused Discussion

Individual reading of best-practice texts represents a third option for beginning the goal-setting process. Pertinent texts include David Booth's and Larry Swartz's *Literacy Techniques* (2004), George Hillocks' *Research on Written Composition: New Directions for Teaching* (1986), and Bess Hinson's *New Directions in Reading Instruction* (2000). Chapters 5 and 6 in this book also address the topic of best practice in reading and writing instruction, respectively. After teachers have read the selected texts, leaders pose this question for discussion: "What does our reading suggest about how we might work together to coordinate literacy instruction in our school?" Invite colleagues to jot notes about their reading before engaging in discussion.

Colleagues might now use a Think-Pair-Share strategy in which participants reflect on their own (Think), then talk to a partner (Pair), and, finally, present their ideas to the larger group (Share). Either the literacy coach or the meeting chairperson lists the suggestions offered by participants on chart paper. Lively discussion follows! Together, the group first determines whether consensus about one or two goals has emerged. If that hurdle has been cleared, they then determine whether sub-groups such as primary, upper elementary, and junior high/middle school teachers will implement the same literacy goal or variations of the goal.

Sometimes, however, groups need to pare down their list of goals from several possibilities to one or two options. In this case, they often take a vote. I have observed goal-setting meetings in which each teacher received two colored dots to place beside the items they saw as high-priority. The ideal scenario, of course, is a workable consensus that is obvious to all participants without the need to vote. Once again, coaches can remind participants that if their top choice is not selected as a program coordination priority, they can still pursue their first choice as a personal professional development goal.

> Coaches can remind participants that if their top choice is not selected as a program coordination priority, they can still pursue their first choice as a personal professional development goal.

A collegial program assessment process, described below, represents yet another way by which colleagues can move from individual reflection to specific collegial goal-setting and planning.

Option 4: Collegial Program Assessment Followed by Focused Discussion

This section presents a reproducible checklist (see pages 26–28) designed to help teachers and literacy coaches assess the current reality of their school's literacy program. This checklist may also prove useful to individual teachers as they reflect on personal professional development priorities. As well, it can help guide groups interested in systematic reflection as part of their goal setting and planning.

Individual teachers may use the checklist to stimulate their thinking in response to five key questions:

1. What are the strengths of my own language arts/literacy program instruction?
2. What goals would I like to achieve in my language arts/literacy program?
3. What personal learning will help me reach my goals?
4. What instructional plans will I implement to achieve my goals and personal learning?
5. How will I assess the instructional benefits to my students?

Groups of teachers may complete the checklist as an early step in goal setting. In completing the checklist, teachers and administrators work together to analyze their global assessment of the school's program rather than the program underway in particular classrooms.

A scheduled time is set aside for participants to complete the checklist, which is formatted as a survey. Each item represents a continuum. Respondents circle a number ranging from 5 to 1 to indicate whether a particular area is perceived as a strength or as an area of need.

The checklist helps to guide individual reflection as part of the goal-setting process. Colleagues fill out the checklist individually. They then meet in a larger group to compare and discuss their responses to arrive at a consensus about which one or two goals to pursue. As part of the focused discussion, the chairperson invites individuals to review their own checklist responses to note patterns and priorities that they can then share in a Think-Pair-Share session. Once everyone in the group has completed the checklist, they can discuss:

- program features that they perceive as strengths within the school
- program features that could become goals for coordinated practice across grades and subject areas

The challenge is to choose only one or two priorities suitable for a school-wide collaborative literacy project.

Using the Literacy Program Assessment Checklist

Some schools have successfully followed these steps when completing their program assessment checklist:

1. Teachers, literacy coaches, and administrators review the purpose of the exercise: individual and group reflection about potential collaborative literacy goals. Colleagues then suggest additions, deletions, and modifications to the assessment checklist. This exercise demonstrates respect for colleagues in the selection and use of relevant program assessment criteria. While reviewing and perhaps revising the program assessment checklist, participants should ask for clarification if the meaning of any item on the checklist is unclear to them.
2. Teachers, literacy coaches, and administrators complete the checklist individually, reflecting on language arts program strengths and needs in the school, *not* in individual classrooms.
3. Teachers, literacy coaches, and administrators meet to compare and discuss their checklist responses. They should always begin by describing program strengths before moving to program needs—*not* program "weaknesses." Teachers often become defensive if program needs are described as weaknesses. Teachers are less likely to become defensive if the accent is placed on student needs rather than on program deficiencies. Acknowledging and celebrating program strengths as the starting point for discussion emphasizes the importance of building on shared accomplishments.

Teachers are less likely to become defensive if the accent is placed on student needs rather than on program deficiencies. Acknowledging and celebrating program strengths as the starting point for discussion emphasizes the importance of building on shared accomplishments.

4. Teachers, literacy coaches, and administrators determine one or two program goals for coordination within the school. The suggestions for building consensus presented earlier in this chapter apply equally to using a program assessment checklist. Teachers may, both individually and collectively, arrive at a wide range of goal-setting priorities. That is why focused discussion is needed to establish the highest priorities for goal setting.

The wisdom of selecting one or two goals rather than a long list applies here as well. While identifying top priorities for program coordination in the coming year, individuals can, at the same time, work together as a group to identify another priority for another year. Colleagues should settle for likely gains linked to a limited number of goals rather than risk failure by selecting too many goals.

Publishing the Final Goal Statement

To conclude the goal-setting process, the literacy coach presents a print copy of the goal statement for colleagues to review, edit, and refine. Some schools use large poster paper to develop and revise their goal statement. Once participants have agreed on wording, colleagues may individually sign a final draft poster version of the goal statement to indicate their personal commitment to the goal (or goals). A goal statement should be brief but clear, as shown in this example:

> This year at Bradford School, we will work together to help students improve their reading ability. We will emphasize students' ability to identify the comprehension strategies they use before, during, and after reading unfamiliar texts in all content areas.

Creating a Sense of Ownership

Some schools display their collaborative goal statement prominently throughout the school. Many schools publish the goal statement in the school newsletter and post it to the school website. At meetings with parents and guardians, principals and literacy coaches lead discussions about how family and community members can help the school meet its goal. Publishing and distributing the goal statement alerts students, family members, and community members of the school's vision for coordinated literacy instruction, designed to benefit all children served by the school.

With guidance from teachers, groups of students could work together to make posters so that the goal(s) are displayed in classrooms, in the school foyer, in the main office, in the resource centre, and in the lunchroom. A handout could be prepared for Parents' Night, and students could make flyers or bookmarks announcing the goal(s) to take home to their families. Students and teachers could collaborate on a marketing/publicity campaign, titled "Our School's Literacy Goal," that would tie in with representing and media literacy as well. Activities such as these create a sense of ownership of the literacy project, both at school and at home.

Publishing and distributing the goal statement alerts students, family members, and community members of the school's vision for coordinated literacy instruction, designed to benefit all children served by the school.

Literacy Program Assessment Checklist

1. *How our school helps students achieve literacy outcomes through a safe, supportive, and productive classroom environment:*

		Program Strength			*Program Need*	
a)	The classroom environment is supportive, with frequent acknowledgement of all students.	5	4	3	2	1
b)	Students are frequently encouraged to value and share personal knowledge, to solve problems, to take risks, and to make independent decisions about their work-in-progress.	5	4	3	2	1
c)	Students frequently confer with teachers and other students about work-in-progress.	5	4	3	2	1
d)	Students work in varied grouping patterns—whole class, small group, and individual learning.	5	4	3	2	1
e)	Students enjoy opportunities to investigate topics, to ask questions, and to present their findings to audiences.	5	4	3	2	1
f)	Students sometimes engage in modified learning activities.	5	4	3	2	1
g)	Students are offered a measure of choice in reading and writing content and in planning projects.	5	4	3	2	1

2. *How our school helps students achieve literacy outcomes through exploratory language and metacognition:*

		Program Strength			*Program Need*	
a)	Students sometimes brainstorm and write notes, including journal and learning log entries, to explore ideas and strategies.	5	4	3	2	1
b)	Students regularly use human resources and technology for help in choosing strategies to complete learning tasks.	5	4	3	2	1
c)	Students frequently express their own interests and preferences in completing tasks.	5	4	3	2	1
d)	Students frequently consider suggestions from others when completing tasks.	5	4	3	2	1
e)	Students regularly set relevant and specific learning goals for themselves.	5	4	3	2	1
f)	Students capably describe their strategies before, during, and after completing learning tasks.	5	4	3	2	1

3. *How our school helps students read well and comprehend print, oral, visual, and media texts:*

		Program Strength			*Program Need*	
a)	Students interpret and evaluate a wide variety of texts, including print, oral, visual, and media texts.	5	4	3	2	1
b)	Students experience a comprehensive reading program that includes independent reading and guided reading.	5	4	3	2	1
c)	Students read for enjoyment at school and at home.	5	4	3	2	1
d)	Students make productive use of school time allowed for reading.	5	4	3	2	1
e)	Students regularly read a variety of complete texts representing different genres.	5	4	3	2	1

	Program Strength			Program Need	
f) Students regularly identify comprehension strategies for interpreting texts, e.g.: questioning, predicting, building background knowledge, visualizing, connecting text to personal experience, and monitoring for understanding.	5	4	3	2	1
g) Students often reread to reconsider their interpretation of a text based on checking for details and engaging in discussion.	5	4	3	2	1
h) Students employ textual evidence to support their interpretations and judgements.	5	4	3	2	1
i) Students engage in reading activities related to clearly defined learning outcomes.	5	4	3	2	1
j) Students talk and write about their connections to new texts as well as to familiar texts and between new texts and familiar personal experiences.	5	4	3	2	1

4. *How our school helps students write well:*

	Program Strength			Program Need	
a) Students use print, media, and human sources to conduct research.	5	4	3	2	1
b) Students employ strategies to gather, record, and organize research information.	5	4	3	2	1
c) Students evaluate the source, relevance, accuracy, and value of research information.	5	4	3	2	1
d) Students frequently write to explore ideas and to develop understanding of new content.	5	4	3	2	1
e) Students write for a variety of purposes and audiences and in a variety of forms.	5	4	3	2	1
f) Students clearly articulate the purpose, the audience, the format, the topic, and the voice they use in writing a composition.	5	4	3	2	1
g) Students engage in appropriate pre-writing activities, such as interviewing, webbing, dramatizing, and making sketches or diagrams.	5	4	3	2	1
h) Students often engage in revision activities with an emphasis on applying specific criteria to revise their writing.	5	4	3	2	1
i) Students frequently present final draft writing to an audience.	5	4	3	2	1
j) Students receive both praise and well-focused, specific suggestions to improve their writing.	5	4	3	2	1
k) Students participate in conferences with both teacher and peers related to work-in-progress.	5	4	3	2	1

5. *How our school helps students achieve oral language outcomes:*

	Program Strength			Program Need	
a) Students and teachers perform and listen to oral language texts (e.g., poetry, plays, Readers' Theatre).	5	4	3	2	1
b) Students often make formal oral presentations to classmates.	5	4	3	2	1
c) Students interpret and assess their classmates' oral presentations.	5	4	3	2	1
d) Students often work collaboratively.	5	4	3	2	1

e) Students assess their own participation in small-group learning tasks.	5	4	3	2	1
f) Students monitor and assess their own listening.	5	4	3	2	1

6. *How our school helps students achieve viewing and representing outcomes:*

	Program Strength			*Program Need*	
a) Students interpret and assess publications, advertisements, films, graphics, cartoons, and other media texts (both print and non-print).	5	4	3	2	1
b) Students dramatize texts for peers and others.	5	4	3	2	1
c) Students creative visual representations, including texts that combine word and image.	5	4	3	2	1
d) Students interpret and assess their own dramatizations and representations and those completed by peers.	5	4	3	2	1

7. *How our school uses planning and assessment to improve students' learning:*

	Program Strength			*Program Need*	
a) Long-range plans outline approximate timelines, themes, or topics; major expectations; principal resources; instructional procedures; and assessment techniques.	5	4	3	2	1
b) Short-range plans outline current work-in-progress; these plans account for timelines, theme, or topic; specific learner expectations; specific resources; specific instructional procedures; and specific evaluation techniques.	5	4	3	2	1
c) Instructional plans sometimes allow students to choose their own assignments.	5	4	3	2	1
d) Instructional plans account for modification of resources and learning activities, modified assessment, and support from the teacher, other adults, and peers.	5	4	3	2	1
e) Students' progress is assessed through a variety of methods: checklists, observation notes, one-on-one conferences, work samples, rubrics, and tests.	5	4	3	2	1
f) Students regularly assess their own work using specific criteria to check for specific features.	5	4	3	2	1
g) Students' assessment includes assessment of oral language and representational tasks.	5	4	3	2	1
h) Students' assessment emphasizes praise and specific feedback for each student in the class.	5	4	3	2	1
i) Students and teachers work together to develop and use rubrics.	5	4	3	2	1
j) Students work with exemplars for both instruction and assessment.	5	4	3	2	1
k) Students' learning includes activities that appeal to varied learning styles: visual, verbal, mathematical, musical, and kinesthetic.	5	4	3	2	1

Checklist for Literacy Coaches and Administrators

Literacy coaches and school administrators may use this checklist to ensure they have met the following criteria in goal setting and planning related to coordinated instructional practice:

☐ We have clearly described a collegial process involving specific timeframes for our collaborative literacy project.

☐ We have consulted with colleagues to determine whether an overview session or individual professional reading about best literacy practice would help us explore options for program coordination and related professional development.

☐ We have guided colleagues toward selection of a manageable number of program coordination goals (one or two specific goals only).

☐ We have presented colleagues with the option of a collegial program assessment checklist as part of the process for making decisions about program coordination goals.

☐ We have distributed a print copy of our school's literacy goal(s) for colleagues to review, edit, and refine.

☐ We have involved colleagues in decision making about implementation strategies, professional development, and assessment related to our goal(s).

☐ We have published and distributed our goal statement to students, families, and the school community.

3

Professional Development and Implementation

An Inquiry Approach to Professional Development

Collegial goal setting based on honest appraisal of a school's current reality is the first step in launching a collaborative literacy project. The process of goal setting leads teachers and literacy coaches to consider two interrelated questions:

1. What is our plan, including a timeline, for implementing the instructional strategies that will help us achieve our collaborative literacy goal?
2. What professional development will help us achieve our shared literacy goal?

Plans for professional development that emerge from the goal-setting phase are carried out during a project's implementation phase. Teachers often discover, however, that the implementation of instructional strategies related to the collaborative goal leads to further questions and concerns. In turn, addressing these questions and concerns can reveal a need for professional development activities that no one had anticipated earlier. What becomes abundantly clear over time is that the interrelationship between implementation and professional development is organic, not prescribed.

As stated earlier, successful collaborative literacy projects involve an inquiry approach. Adopting an inquiry approach links implementation of the targeted instructional strategies in the classroom to professional development. An inquiry approach involves asking reflective questions about how to blend professional development into daily teaching and learning activities in order to achieve the school's literacy goal. After the initial goal-setting phase of a collaborative project, colleagues meet to discuss questions such as:

> An inquiry approach involves asking reflective questions about how to blend professional development into daily teaching and learning activities in order to achieve the school's literacy goal.

*   What do we need to learn to implement our collaborative literacy goal?
*   What instructional strategies can we implement to meet our goal?
*   How might we adapt these strategies to meet the needs of all children served by our school?
*   What questions and concerns do we have about these instructional strategies?
*   What resources will we need to implement our goal?
*   What is our timeline for classroom implementation of selected instructional strategies?
*   How will we assess these strategies' benefits to students?
*   How will we involve students, family members, and the community beyond the school in helping us achieve our collaborative literacy goal?

When teachers adopt an inquiry approach to professional development, they return to these questions regularly as they implement and refine selected instructional strategies. Sometimes teachers arrange a session to discuss these questions with the team's literacy coach. They also engage in informal conversations with colleagues. They might add the questions to the agenda of a regularly scheduled meeting. As well, they might pursue answers to the questions through individual professional development. As mentioned earlier, adequate time for meetings and for professional development activities is essential to ensure a successful collaborative literacy project.

Planning Effective School-Based Professional Development

An inquiry approach to professional development guides teachers toward a range of professional development options. It is common and acceptable for individual teachers to select different options. Typically, teachers begin to weigh possibilities for professional development from the time they select their school's collaborative literacy goal. During the implementation phase, they explore the "how" of professional development along with the "what." In accordance with an inquiry model, teachers ponder questions such as, "How can I most effectively learn about instructional strategies related to our collaborative literacy goal?" While presentations given by experts are often worth attending, teachers need to explore other kinds of professional development as well, for example:

- Completing courses, including on-line courses, and sharing new ideas with colleagues
- Attending workshops or conferences or viewing webcasts and reporting back to colleagues
- Observing a colleague model an instructional strategy in a classroom
- Reading professional literature followed by discussion or sharing in a study group
- Mentoring
- Peer partnerships focused on development of instructional resources (Jennifer Allen's *Becoming a Literacy Leader* [2006] features excellent scenarios depicting peer partnerships in action.)
- Collegial creation of instructional resources
- Group assessment of student work to establish standards of achievement

The final two bulleted items receive further attention in this book. Creation of instructional resources is discussed later in this chapter. Group marking is discussed in Chapter 6.

Levels of Professional Development Effectiveness

No matter what type of professional development activity is undertaken, its effectiveness can be gauged by its impact on classroom practice and, ultimately, by its benefits in terms of student learning and achievement.

More than one teacher has lamented having to sit through yet another presentation with no hint of practical classroom application. What are the hallmarks of highly effective versus less effective professional development? What constitutes the highest level of professional development? No matter what type of professional development activity is undertaken, its effectiveness can be gauged by its impact on classroom practice and, ultimately, by its benefits in terms of student learning and achievement. The final section of this chapter features a real-life example of how a group of Grade 3 students benefited from their teachers' professional development.

The following chart presents levels of professional development effectiveness related to classroom implementation.

PROFESSIONAL DEVELOPMENT EFFECTIVENESS

Level 0	No value	Professional development fails to influence classroom practice.
Level 1	Acceptable Value	Professional development leads teachers to implement an instructional strategy.
Level 2	High Value	Professional development results in teachers creating their own instructional material related to their learning.
Level 3	Maximum Value	Professional development results in teachers sharing instructional material (which they have developed themselves) with colleagues in and beyond the school.

At Level 1, teachers take something back to their classrooms that they learned as a result of professional development. Effective school-based professional development supports practice consistent with Level 1 while at the same time encouraging teachers to attain the higher values of Levels 2 and 3. As a follow-up to professional development, literacy coaches invite colleagues to discuss their classroom implementation: What instructional strategies have they tried and modified? What worked well and what didn't work well?

Attaining Level 2 is especially commendable because this form of professional development demonstrates a higher level of commitment to excellence than simply implementing a strategy suggested by someone else. At Level 2, teachers are so convinced of the value of the instructional strategies they have learned about that they spend time planning and developing their own related instructional resources.

Commitment and action at Level 2 apply to both individual and collegial professional development. However, there is exponentially added value with regard to the latter. Through collegial development of instructional material, teachers demonstrate that they truly value coordinated practice to benefit all students served by the school. Teachers typically report deep professional satisfaction in working collegially to prepare, implement, and refine their own instructional material.

> Through collegial development of instructional material, teachers demonstrate that they truly value coordinated practice to benefit all students served by the school.

Examples of Level 2 professional development are becoming increasingly evident in schools. For example, many schools set aside time for teachers to collaborate to develop assessment rubrics for writing. Working together to develop rubrics signals that colleagues share an understanding of the effectiveness of valid criteria in enhancing students' writing. To extend the effectiveness of rubrics even further, many schools allot time for teachers to select exemplars of student writing to demonstrate standards of achievement at different grades.

Typically, elementary teachers select high, average, and low samples of narrative writing at each grade level. Then, they extend the collection beyond narrative writing to other forms of writing, such as description or exposition. These exemplar collections are photocopied and shared among colleagues. Through the standard-setting process, teachers gain confidence in their grasp of expectations related to student achievement at different grade levels.

Benefits of Creating and Sharing Resources

Educators confronting the realities of attrition and staff turnover recognize another benefit of Level 2 professional development. Instructional resources created by colleagues represent a valuable gift to new teachers joining a staff. The resources *show* rather than *tell about* the school's priorities for program coordination. A new teacher can use these resources to guide his or her practice. Working alongside a literacy coach or a mentor, a new teacher can build upon the resources to plan instruction with confidence.

To cite one example, a beginning teacher I once worked with had received a collection of grade-level exemplars for writing. This collection, representing high, average, and low samples for typical grade-level writing tasks, was published as part of a school's program coordination plan. The teacher reported that the collection helped her understand grade-level expectations in a way that legal program documents never could. The "showing" of expectations in the exemplars communicated information to her more clearly than the "telling" of expectations in the program document.

Retirement, resignations, and staff transfers in and out of a school are so regular that without a commitment to the collegial creation and collection of instructional resources, a staff will always be starting its program coordination from scratch.

Level 3 professional development is characterized by the sharing of the instructional resources developed by a team with audiences beyond the school. While this level is not *required* for effective school-based collaborative literacy projects, it is always a desirable option. Teachers are no different from other people in their need for praise and recognition. In presenting their material to colleagues, in modeling use of the material with students, or in publishing their material, teachers reinforce the fact that the best learning is learning that is generously shared with others. This behavior signals teachers' interest in learning from other professionals to refine instructional practice in their school.

Level 3 professional development results in activities such as presentations at conferences, sharing sessions or videoconferencing with other schools, and publication in professional journals or on websites. Local chapters of organizations such as the International Reading Association and the National Council of Teachers of English welcome submissions to their publications.

Potential Pitfalls

As literacy coaches and principals nudge colleagues toward high levels of professional development effectiveness, they must take the potential pitfalls into account. What happens if an external audience for a presentation by a school's teachers reacts negatively to the presentation? As a speaker at numerous conventions, conferences, and workshops, I know that some teachers can be critical of their peers. Speakers must always be prepared for a negative response from some members of an audience.

> In presenting their material to colleagues, in modeling use of the material with students, or in publishing their material, teachers reinforce the fact that the best learning is learning that is generously shared with others.

Ideally, presenters use feedback, including negative feedback, as a learning opportunity. In presenting instructional material that they have developed to other teachers in and beyond the school, teachers should view feedback as an opportunity to refine the material. Feedback helps them to reflect on questions such as, "How can our presentation and audience reactions to it help us improve our instructional material?"

Teachers report another common pitfall related to the development of instructional material. After hours of work creating material, it can sit and "gather dust." In my experience, this situation is most typical of coordination projects that have been organized, often by a school district's central office, without the involvement of teachers in collaborative goal setting.

Yet another problem stems from the fact that school districts and schools sometimes distribute packages of instructional material developed by teachers with insufficient professional development support. Within schools, this material may be passed on to a newly hired colleague without someone taking time to explain and offer classroom modeling of the instructional strategies.

For successful implementation of school-developed instructional material, literacy coaches, principals, and school district leaders should always plan professional development sessions that feature an active workshop approach. Allow the audience time to explore and assess the material by means of active learning. Such learning can take the form of:

- role-playing
- trying out new activities
- talking to a partner about potential uses of the material
- discussing possible modifications of the material with members of a small group
- sharing discoveries made in small groups with the larger group

When teachers are invited to "play" with the material in small groups, they are much more likely to implement it. In addition, literacy coaches should always offer ample time and attention to newly appointed staff members. A coach must take time to explain and promote the material, to invite questions and expressions of concern, and to encourage new teachers to ask for help when they need it. Otherwise, passing on material will have minimal impact.

A final concern regarding the distribution of instructional material prepared by teachers is that the material might become outdated. This is especially true of standard-setting exemplar collections. Teachers have told me that their work in selecting exemplars to demonstrate expectations results in higher standards over time. Teachers' shared understanding of expectations and their ongoing collaboration with each other yield improvements in students' writing—and standards rise. Literacy coaches should encourage colleagues to review instructional material that they have created, to update it when necessary, and to discard it when it becomes out of date. They must ensure that only current, program-specific instructional resources are shared with colleagues.

No matter what the level of professional development achieved in a school, literacy coaches must schedule time for colleagues to discuss their implementation of instructional strategies. How will teachers share their implementation stories? Will they tell their stories in a literacy team meeting? Will they present lesson material to colleagues? Will they work together to create instructional resources? Are they open to presenting materials to audiences beyond the

Scheduling time for ongoing discussion of implementation strategies is the foundation for effective collaborative literacy projects.

school? Scheduling time for ongoing discussion of implementation strategies is the foundation for effective collaborative literacy projects.

Encouraging Expression of Concerns

From the outset of professional development planning, literacy leaders should recognize that teachers will vary in their enthusiasm and commitment to a collegial coordination plan. One critical safeguard is to encourage teachers to express their concerns throughout the project. The Concerns-Based Adoption Model (Loucks-Horsley, 1996) stresses that teachers typically ask how any innovation or plan will affect them personally. What will they have to learn to implement change? Literacy coaches encourage articulation of concerns so that professional development and discussion can help resolve those concerns. By regularly inviting teachers to voice their frustrations, leaders demonstrate that they care about helping teachers deal with implementation hurdles. Ongoing professional development sessions focus on suggestions related to teachers' concerns. Sometimes literacy coaches help teachers address concerns by one-on-one consultation or by modeling instructional strategies for them.

At regular intervals, literacy coaches should encourage teachers to respond to the prompt, "When I think about our current literacy coordination plan, I am now concerned about…." In meetings and professional development sessions, literacy coaches should post teachers' concerns and conclude each session with a discussion of how to address them.

Benefiting Students

I have often seen the beneficial effects on students of an inquiry approach and an emphasis on high-level professional development. For example, one school selected as its collaborative literacy goal an improvement in students' ability to identify and employ writing strategies. The school's Grade 3 teachers were concerned that much of their students' writing lacked fluency. Also, students' written text lacked detail. Students took a long time to write very little.

The teachers' concern led them to seek out instructional suggestions that would benefit their students. As is typical of an inquiry approach, the teachers shared ideas about instructional strategies and sought advice from other colleagues. Ongoing discussion led them to a rich professional development resource, *Reclaiming Reluctant Writers*, by Kellie Buis (2007). The teachers agreed that an excellent pre-writing strategy that Buis recommended for narrative writing, called "Story Bones," might work well with their students. A graphic organizer featuring the Story Bones approach appears on the following page. (A full-size version of this graphic organizer for classroom use appears in the Appendices at the back of this book.)

The teachers engaged students in a variety of learning activities related to the Story Bones strategy. These activities included oral storytelling using Story Bones; acting out skits based on Story Bones; discussing the Story Bones elements in stories they had read recently; and so on. Teachers then invited students to use Story Bones in their own writing.

This instructional approach posed the usual implementation challenges. For example, the first time students tried this pre-writing strategy, a few students planned a story using the Story Bones framework—and then proceeded to write a totally different story! Nevertheless, over time, teachers began to notice the beneficial effects of Story Bones. More and more students began to establish, develop, and resolve conflicts in their narrative compositions. Students learned to transform their thin texts into more robust pieces of writing.

Story Bones

Story: _____

Author: _____

Main character: _____

Problem starts when _____

_____

After that _____

_____

Next _____

_____

Then _____

_____

Problem is solved when _____

_____

Ending _____

_____

Adapted from *Reclaiming Reluctant Writers*, page 50, by Kellie Buis (Pembroke Publishers, 2007). Permission to copy for classroom use. Pembroke Publishers.

Subsequently, as part of their professional development related to their work with Story Bones, the teachers shared ideas about revision strategies that would work well with their students.

After reviewing several rubrics developed by other educators, the teachers collaborated to develop the story writing rubric shown on the following page. Note its student-friendly language. This rubric clearly benefited student writers as they revised their stories on their own and with help from their peers.

The students taught by these teachers grew as writers because their teachers engaged in an inquiry approach to professional development related to the school's collaborative literacy goal. Students benefited because their teachers felt confident in voicing their concerns about their students' writing and in seeking advice to address those concerns. Most importantly, students benefited because their teachers created instructional material *with students in mind*.

Students benefited because their teachers created instructional material *with students in mind*.

Story Writing Rubric

	I'm not there yet	I'm getting there	I'm there now
Content (Snappy ideas and clear, interesting details)	When someone reads my writing, they have a lot of questions because they are not sure what I mean. My details are not clear to them.	Most of my writing is clear. I have some interesting details but I need to add more.	My writing is clear to the reader. I have included interesting details that make the reader want to keep reading.
Organization (Beginning, middle, and ending)	My writing confuses the reader about the story's problem, solution, and ending.	My writing sometimes clearly builds to a problem, then builds to a solution, and then has an ending.	My writing clearly builds to a problem, then builds to a solution to the problem, and then has an ending.
Sentence structure (Complete/Varied sentences)	Most of my sentences are not complete. I always write the same type of sentence.	I sometimes write complete sentences. I use one or two different types of sentences.	I always write complete sentences. I use three or more different types of sentences.
Word choice (Words that show rather than tell)	The reader often asks, "What does this word mean?"	My words are ordinary but sometimes they show the reader what I mean.	I often choose the right words to show the reader what I mean.
Conventions (Spelling, grammar, and punctuation)	I have made so many mistakes that my reader gets confused. I miss many needed corrections in my editing.	I miss quite a few needed corrections in my editing.	I make most of the needed corrections in my editing.

Documenting Collaborative Literacy Projects

Throughout a collaborative literacy project, colleagues make many decisions and literacy coaches document these decisions, including those concerning timelines. Often, school district authorities ask for a copy of this information. More importantly, literacy coaches share the documentation with colleagues. The documentation shows educators and others in the school community how all aspects of the project—goal setting, professional development, implementation, and assessment—are coherently connected. The following pages illustrate a collaborative project record maintained by a literacy coach. (A blank version of this "Literacy Project Implementation Plan" appears on pages 94–95 in the Appendices at the back of this book). The literacy coach ensures that colleagues always have access to the most up-to-date version of the plan. Sometimes, coaches post the plan prominently or store it in a binder.

This chapter has examined how literacy coaches can support teachers in using an inquiry approach in order to progress from the exploration of possibilities for professional development to specific plans for implementation. As colleagues reach consensus about responses to the questions they raise, coaches document the group's planning decisions and share meeting notes and timelines among all participants. This documentation will help ensure that there are no surprises and no misunderstandings later on.

Chapter 4 outlines the fourth and final key aspect of a collaborative literacy project: assessment.

Literacy Project Implementation Plan

School: __Allen Road School__

Timeframe for Project: ___September, 2008–June, 2009___

Participants in Project: __Grades 3-6 Teachers, Principal, School Librarian,__

___Teacher Assistants, Parent Volunteers___

Goal-Setting Activities and Dates	Goal Statement
1. Start-up Meeting: Presentation re. potential of the literacy project, review of data about our current school population, teacher assessment data, standardized test data, review of district funding guidelines; brief overview of process and resources available for project—Sept. 15	Across grades and subject areas at Allen Road School, we will work to improve students' ability to identify and use writing strategies from pre-writing through to revision.
2. Goal-Setting Meeting: Review and selection of goal-setting options—Sept. 22	
3. Focused discussion following individual completion of program assessment checklist. Note that discussion indicated growing consensus related to a writing project—Sept. 29	
4. Presentation on Best Practice in Writing with a focus on revision—Oct. 4	
5. Development of Goal Statement—Oct. 6	
6. Distribution of print copies of Goal Statement—Oct.10	

Plan to Publicize Goal
1. Item in school newsletter: information about project, invitation to meeting re. parents'/guardians' participation in project—Oct. 17
2. Presentation at School Council Meeting featuring a video of students talking about why writing is important. Focus: What parents/guardians can do to encourage and help improve their children's writing—Oct. 25

Professional Development	Implementation Strategies	Assessment Plan
1. Literacy coach orders professional books and materials related to project—Oct. 18 2. Literacy coach reviews information about professional resources available in the school and district: books, journals, DVDs, human resources—Nov. 17 3. Three teachers attend a workshop on use of exemplars to improve student writing—Nov. 24 4. Two teachers attend a workshop on improving language conventions in student writing—Jan. 17 5. Literacy coach meets with librarian, teacher assistants, and adult volunteers to review their role in the project (ongoing)	1. Teachers work with a partner to review and invite feedback about two plans for writing assignments that they will develop to emphasize strategies—Nov. 1-Apr. 30. Meeting time allowed for the work. 2. Teachers work individually, with a partner, or in a small group to develop instructional material related to writing strategies—Feb. 2 (Professional Day). 3. Teachers informally arrange visits to observe colleagues throughout the project. **Meeting Times** _____ _____ _____ _____ _____ _____ _____ _____ (Early dismissal allowed for Friday meetings)	1. Students will complete a different but similar writing-prompt assignment in October and May. A teacher committee will develop the prompt and select the scoring rubric. When they have completed their writing, students will complete a survey to report on strategies they used before, during, and after writing. 2. Following agreement about scoring procedures, writing samples and survey forms will be scored on November and May Professional Days. **Learning From Assessment** 1. The literacy coach gathers assessment information. Colleagues assess the level of improvement in the writing tests and in student ability to identify writing strategies.—May 18/25 meetings 2. Literacy coach drafts and vets assessment report—June 1.

Checklist for Literacy Coaches and Administrators

Literacy coaches and administrators may use this checklist to ensure they have met the following criteria in planning implementation and professional development related to the school's program coordination goal(s):

☐ We have emphasized an inquiry approach to professional development that challenges teachers to pose questions, to seek answers through professional development, and to select and refine appropriate implementation strategies.

☐ We have encouraged teachers to select from a range of professional development options related to our program coordination goals.

☐ We have helped colleagues to select implementation strategies related to our coordination goal and to set realistic timelines for implementation.

☐ We have engaged colleagues in discussions to assess the effectiveness of instructional strategies implemented in the collaboration project.

☐ We have distributed print copies of agreements about implementation strategies and timelines.

☐ We have encouraged colleagues to create instructional material related to our program coordination goals.

☐ We have encouraged teachers to share instructional material with colleagues in and beyond the school through workshops, presentations, and publications.

☐ We regularly encourage teachers to express concerns about implementation of instructional strategies related to program goals and we work together to address those concerns.

4

Assessing Collaborative Literacy Projects

Gathering and Analyzing Assessment Data

The goal setting, professional development, and implementation of instruction that evolve as a collaborative literacy project unfolds are all linked to the selection of appropriate assessment strategies. Many jurisdictions stipulate that gathering assessment data is a condition for funding school-based literacy projects. Even if assessment has not been mandated, however, literacy coaches should encourage teachers to view assessment as a valuable opportunity to gauge the breadth and depth of students' learning.

At the same time, administrators and literacy coaches must recognize that teachers are sometimes nervous about gathering assessment data. Teachers may feel that it is their teaching skill rather than the effectiveness of the instructional strategies that is being assessed. Nonetheless, unless relevant assessment data are gathered and analyzed, how will colleagues judge the efficacy of their implementation strategies?

Administrators and coaches should make clear that assessment is designed to measure the effectiveness of the instructional strategies related to the project goal. Assessment also paves the way for subsequent refinement of those strategies in order to benefit students.

> Administrators and coaches should make clear that assessment is designed to measure the effectiveness of the instructional strategies related to the project goal. Assessment also paves the way for subsequent refinement of those strategies in order to benefit students.

Matching Assessment to the Literacy Goal

How can literacy coaches advocate the collection of assessment data and at the same time dispel teachers' apprehensions about assessment? One step in the right direction is to honour the following principle: *Teachers must ensure that the assessment data they gather are appropriate to both the literacy project goal and to the instructional strategies aligned with the goal.*

As a general rule, in most school-based literacy projects, ongoing data gathered by teachers, including performance assessments of student work, are more relevant than standardized test data. While standardized test data may sometimes influence the choice of project goal and the direction a project takes, colleagues cannot assume that test scores are always the preferred or exclusive measure of program effectiveness. Once again, colleagues should work together to determine precisely which assessment data might be appropriate for their collaborative goal. They then decide how to collect and interpret that data.

Examples of Relevant Assessment Data

I once worked with a group of teachers who were striving to increase the amount of reading for enjoyment completed by their students. The teachers collaborated to determine how to assess students' progress in attaining this literacy goal. They eventually decided to analyze personal reading lists kept by students, as well as student reading profiles that teachers collected three times during the course of the project. The teachers worked together to develop a consistent approach to their analysis of the personalized reading lists. They also focused on student ability to respond reasonably to each item in the reading profile. An example of a student reading profile appears on the following page.

The teachers in the group assessed their students' ability to fill in specific and appropriate responses to the prompts in the profile. They also averaged the reading rate information that students reported in item 3. In addition, teachers used independent reading records to assess the amount of reading that students had completed. (An example of an independent reading record appears in Chapter 5.) When the project ended, teachers were satisfied that they had selected an appropriate method of gathering assessment data related to their literacy goal. An analysis of the students' reading lists, reading profiles, and independent reading records provided clear evidence that students were reading more texts for enjoyment more often, compared to their prior reading behavior.

As another example, a group of colleagues decided to collaborate to improve students' competence in employing the higher-level thinking skills of inference and evaluation. (Chapter 5 explores this project in greater depth.) The teachers worked together to develop grade-level reading tests that included inferential and evaluative questions. They administered the same test in early October and then in late May to track the level of student improvement. The teachers also factored in standardized reading test data (based on a province-wide achievement test). However, they placed greater emphasis—and appropriately so—on the gains in student competence revealed by the parallel pre-project and post-project tests they had administered.

Collaborative literacy projects that aim to improve students' writing ability logically involve the collection of a prescribed number of writing samples, usually at the beginning and at the end of the project. Teachers decide whether the writing will occur within the framework of a timed test in response to a prompt, or whether the samples will emerge from student work-in-progress examined both early and late in the project. Teachers collaborate to select or create a rubric to assess the writing samples. They use the rubric to record the level of improvement in students' mastery of a particular trait or form of writing.

As yet another example of how to determine relevant assessment data, a group of colleagues focused on the goal of improving their students' ability to work productively in small groups. The team members developed an assessment form that students completed four times during the literacy project. (The form is reproduced on page 46.)

In analyzing students' responses to the items on the form, teachers completed two tasks:

- counting and averaging check marks
- counting the number of students who specified a goal for improved small-group work

Collaborative literacy projects that aim to improve students' writing ability logically involve the collection of a prescribed number of writing samples, usually at the beginning and at the end of the project.

My Current Reading Profile

Name: _____ Date: _____

1. I like books that are _____

_____

_____ .

2. I dislike books that are _____

_____

_____ .

3. I usually read a book in _____ days/weeks.

4. When I describe myself as a reader, I use phrases such as _____

_____

_____

_____

_____ .

5. I would like to read more about_____

_____

_____

_____

_____ .

6. For the next month, my personal reading goal is to _____

_____

_____

_____

_____ .

Student Self-Assessment Form for Small-Group Work

Name: _____

Due Date: _____

Group Members: _____

_____

Please place a check mark beside each statement that accurately describes you.

Criteria	My New Goal(s) for Small-Group Work
_____ 1. I helped my group review its task. Our task was to _____ _____ _____	_____ _____ _____
_____ 2. I contributed relevant ideas; I stayed on topic. One idea that I contributed was _____ _____	_____ _____ _____
_____ 3. I listened carefully and respectfully to other group members. I wondered about _____ _____	_____ _____ _____
_____ 4. I was open-minded about different interpretations or understandings. I wondered about_____ _____ _____	_____ _____ _____ _____
_____ 5. I helped my group stay focused on its task by using polite reminders.	_____ _____ _____
_____ 6. I contributed to the summary that we wrote to conclude our group work. We concluded that _____ _____ _____	_____ _____ _____
_____ 7. I encouraged all members of the group to contribute.	_____ _____

Teachers charted student progress during the four times they used the checklist and reported that the checklist clearly helped students work more productively in small groups. One teacher observed that improved listening and speaking skills in small groups benefited students in many reading and writing tasks, such as peer editing and planning a Readers' Theatre presentation. The higher scores in the fourth trial signaled definite student progress.

Which Types of Assessment Make Sense?

When determining which types of assessment would work best to track their literacy project goal, colleagues might review the following three general assessment categories, along with the examples of assessment tools listed in the chart below. Teachers and literacy coaches must ask themselves: "Which of these general assessment categories and which assessment tools within each category would best suit our collaborative literacy goal?"

Type of Assessment	Definition	Examples of Assessment Tools
Observation	Informal, sometimes casual assessment of students; teachers observe selected students on a given day	• anecdotal records • observations of students working in groups • checklists
Pre-specified Response	Assessment that requires students to approximate a predetermined response	• multiple choice questions • short answer questions • true/false questions • matching questions • dictation tasks • numeric responses to math or science questions
Performance Assessment	Formal assessment that requires the use of criteria that are communicated directly to learners and used as guidelines by both students and teachers	• rubrics for writing and representing • rubrics for projects, research, experimental design, role play, debate, and so on

Besides facilitating appropriate assessment choices, literacy coaches help colleagues plot timelines showing key dates for the collection of assessment data related to their collaborative literacy goal. Equally important, coaches document and distribute print copies of agreements and timelines that reflect the group's decisions about assessment. In my consulting work, I have noted that documenting and posting "We agree…" statements underlines their importance and reminds colleagues of their commitment to the project on a day-to-day basis.

Learning From Assessment Data

When a collaborative literacy project ends, literacy coaches arrange time for teachers to discuss what they have learned from the assessment data they have gathered. Which instructional strategies have been affirmed? Which instructional practices could be improved? What can teachers do to improve their instructional practices?

Literacy coaches guide their colleagues' discussion toward analysis of how shared goals and coordinated instructional practice have affected assessment results. Typically, bright students shine in assessment opportunities. However, documenting program coordination benefits to struggling or average students should be the primary goal of assessment data collection. After all, enhanced student learning is the whole point of program coordination. To emphasize this point, administrators and literacy coaches usually organize some form of celebration at the conclusion of a collaborative literacy project. The celebration highlights how everyone's learning has improved as a result of coaching and collaboration.

A Success Story

My most powerful memory of learning from assessment data is associated with a school in which all Grades 4 to 6 teachers selected a project goal related to reading comprehension. The teachers decided to work together to improve their students' ability to identify reading comprehension strategies for before, during, and after reading an assigned unfamiliar text. (Chapter 5 describes the professional development learning about reading strategies that team members acquired and shared as they pursued this goal.)

At the beginning of the project, teachers asked individual students to complete a form to report on the specific comprehension strategies they used before, during, and after they read a selected unfamiliar text. Teachers chose a different text for each of Grades 4, 5, and 6. Few students could identify even a single strategy! Following structured professional development that centred on reading comprehension and the construction of a shared language to describe comprehension strategies, teachers regularly modeled these strategies for their students. They engaged children in identifying and labeling the reading strategies they were using to understand an unfamiliar text.

At the end of the project, students again completed a form to report on the comprehension strategies they used before, during, and after reading a selected unfamiliar text. Not surprisingly, students demonstrated increased awareness and use of reading comprehension strategies compared to their earlier performance.

In follow-up discussions about the assessment data they had gathered, teachers marveled at how students' thinking diverged widely in identifying the strategies that worked best for them. What the teachers learned from the assessment data confirmed their beliefs about the importance of differentiated instruction. Students benefit by learning and applying the strategies that work best for them. Teachers also noted that students used idiosyncratic language to describe reading comprehension strategies. In an example later in this chapter, a Grade 5 student used the words "make pictures in my mind" even though her teacher consistently used the term "visualizing" to describe this reading strategy. The important point is that the student had internalized an understanding of the

What the teachers learned from the assessment data confirmed their beliefs about the importance of differentiated instruction. Students benefit by learning and applying the strategies that work best for them.

strategy of visualizing and how she could apply it to help her comprehend and connect with text.

In their follow-up discussions as well, some teachers commented that students' comprehension of unfamiliar texts had been strengthened as a result of their improved knowledge and application of reading comprehension strategies. One teacher suggested that, in a future literacy project, the group could focus on documenting the link between reading strategies and skills such as identifying the author's purpose, inferring themes, inferring character traits, and determining word meanings in context.

One notable finding related to student attentiveness to the task at hand. Some teachers pointed out that students managed their time better when they became familiar with the range of reading strategy options available to them. Student thinking about questions such as: "What strategies will I use before I start reading?" helped them settle down to the task and use their time more productively.

Through discussion and reflection on their own learning, these colleagues confirmed and extended their understanding of the importance of reading comprehension strategies as they moved on to consider other options for professional development.

While working with the teachers on this project, I confirmed and extended my own learning about the power of teaching explicit reading comprehension strategies. My experience may be germane to principals, vice principals, and literacy coaches. Everyone who participates in a collaborative literacy project learns something new. At the time the project was underway, I was writing the manuscript for *Language Arts Idea Bank* (2003). I chose the written response of one student participant in the literacy project to illustrate to literacy teachers the value of helping students identify and apply the reading strategies that work best for them. The student's response is reproduced on the following page. (A blank version of the graphic organizer that the student used appears in the Appendices at the back of this book.)

> Everyone who participates in a collaborative literacy project learns something new.

Understanding Myself as a Reader

Name: _____ Date: _____

Title of Text: <u>Pioneering by Lake Ontario by Catherine Traill</u>

Strategies I used before reading:

<u>Before reading a story I look at the picture and make another picture in my mind that</u>
<u>excites me.</u>

Strategies I used during reading:

<u>When I read I usually make pictures in my mind and picture myself being a character in</u>
<u>the story. I also predict what will happen next and how the person feels.</u>

Strategies I used after reading:

<u>After reading I think of more content for the story or a better ending for the story.</u>

My goals for future reading:

<u>I want to read more adventurous books and I want to read longer, more exciting books.</u>

What I have learned about myself as a reader:

<u>I like to read people's lifelong story and how people have to survive. I also like books</u>
<u>with exciting twists at the end.</u>

Reflecting, Sharing, and Celebrating

In reflecting upon and learning from assessment data, colleagues should consider whether the publication of their assessment information would benefit colleagues beyond the school. Assessment analysis that documents student learning is a useful complement to instructional material that teachers have developed as part of their literacy project. Team members could append assessment information when they publish and present the instructional material they have developed together. (Recall how the previous chapter advocated publication and presentation of teachers' own instructional material as representing the highest level of professional development.)

Similarly, literacy coaches can encourage their colleagues to consider how to share the learning derived from assessment data with students and their families. What kinds of action do the assessment results suggest family members might take to help improve their children's reading, writing, viewing, and representing?

In what kinds of literacy-focused discussions and activities could family members participate at home?

Students and their family members could read newspaper headlines together, make predictions about the content of the articles, and then read the articles to confirm or revise their predictions. They could examine labels on food products, ads on TV, or billboards in their neighborhood and then discuss the messages communicated by the many media texts we encounter every day.

Encourage students to use what they have learned in class to present a book talk at home. Also, households could organize a "Family Reading Night" or a "Spotlight on Reading" session once a week in which they share observations about their favorite books, magazines, or other texts and what they'd like to read next.

When reporting to parents and guardians about improved student ability to identify and use writing strategies, one school offered a parent's workshop that featured suggestions for:

- encouraging students to write in their daily lives: notes, letters, e-mails, diary entries, and so on
- sharing writing with family members and displaying it at home
- emphasizing praise rather than criticism
- encouraging children to talk about their thinking before, during, and after they write something

In reporting to parents and guardians about improved student ability to identify and use reading strategies, another school published a school newsletter article that stressed the academic benefits to children when they:

- see important people in their lives reading and talking about their favorite texts
- listen to stories being read aloud
- receive books from others, pick out their own books, and have access to library collections
- are encouraged to talk about their own favorite texts

Concluding a Literary Project

When concluding a literacy project, team members must address two final questions:

1. How can we "package" what we have learned by gathering and analyzing assessment data and publicizing our learning within the school community?
2. How can we celebrate everyone's contribution to a successful literacy project?

Working together to answer these questions wraps up the project on a high note, leading to a consolidation of shared learning and a lasting sense of accomplishment.

Checklist for Literacy Coaches and Administrators

Literacy coaches and administrators may use this checklist to ensure they have met the following criteria in gathering assessment data related to their collaborative literacy project:

☐ We have clearly explained the importance of relevant assessment data pertaining to our collaborative literacy goal.

☐ We have helped colleagues select types of assessment and assessment tools that are appropriate to our collaborative literacy goal.

☐ We have helped colleagues set timelines related to the collection of assessment data.

☐ We have allowed time for colleagues to discuss and celebrate what they have learned from assessment data.

☐ We have encouraged colleagues to publish an analysis of assessment data for audiences beyond the school.

☐ We have publicized our collaborative literacy project and celebrated its success with students' family members and with the school community.

5

Collaborative Projects in Reading Instruction

Why Focus on Reading and Writing?

Chapters 5 and 6 examine program coordination related to best practice in reading and writing instruction, respectively. Why do so many school-based literacy teams choose to coordinate best practice in reading and writing instruction? After all, reading and writing are only two of the six language arts, which also comprise speaking, listening, viewing, and representing.

The answer lies partly in the fact that, in all jurisdictions, reading and writing outcomes typically receive the most pronounced emphasis in prescribed English Language Arts program documents. Furthermore, best practice in reading and writing instruction naturally integrates all six of the language arts. And, finally, program documents that emphasize language across the curriculum—that is, instruction in language skills in subject areas other than language arts—also tend to stress reading and writing. Thus, collaborative literacy projects often emphasize reading and writing as a reflection of the emphasis in prescribed curriculum documents.

Choosing a Best-Practice Goal for Reading Instruction

It falls to literacy coaches to encourage their colleagues to review a range of options before they select a specific goal related to best practice in reading instruction. As part of their responsibility, literacy coaches pre-screen a treasure trove of professional literature pertaining to best practice in teaching reading. They share their knowledge, expertise, and professional reading with colleagues as they work together to establish a shared goal and an implementation plan for a reading-focused literacy project. A collaborative project focused on reading will align with one of the following best-practice goals:

1. Improve students' reading ability by promoting frequent independent reading
2. Improve students' reading ability by coordinating instruction in reading comprehension strategies
3. Improve students' reading ability by emphasizing higher-level thinking skills
4. Improve students' reading ability through activities that incorporate close reading of texts

5. Improve students' reading ability through powerful culminating tasks or extension activities: rich, multi-sensory activities that follow class study of a text or a collection of texts

This chapter intentionally avoids detailed discussion of common methods by which teachers organize reading instruction in their classrooms, for example, shared reading, guided reading, literature circles, and Readers' Workshop. Shared reading is favored by primary teachers and English as a Second Language teachers. In shared reading, students follow along and chime in as a teacher reads a text aloud. The text is often a "big book" that is clearly visible to all students. In guided reading—common in upper elementary and secondary classrooms—teachers model their own reading strategies in a think-aloud and direct students' attention to particular elements of a selected text before, during, and after reading. Literature circles involve the assignment of different roles to students (such as Discussion Director, Illustrator, and Summarizer) as they read and respond to a text as a group. Readers' Workshop features a structured approach based on independent reading and differentiated tasks.

Generally, most teachers adopt an eclectic approach to reading instruction, mixing and matching various methods to suit the needs of all learners. All reading methodologies can embrace any and all of the best-practice goals listed above. Therefore, colleagues can work together to coordinate instruction in ways that respect teachers' individual choices and preferences regarding organization of their reading program.

> Colleagues can work together to coordinate instruction in ways that respect teachers' individual choices and preferences regarding organization of their reading program.

Promoting Frequent Independent Reading

Students become adept in a particular skill set when they have many opportunities to practice in a risk-free environment. Professional literature such as *New Directions in Reading Instruction* (Hinson, 2000) underscores the fact that frequent independent reading results in improved reading comprehension. Many school-based literacy projects aim to increase the amount of independent reading completed by students. Coordinated instructional practice aimed at promoting frequent independent reading honours these principles:

1. Programs emphasize reading for enjoyment or recreational reading.
2. Programs help students set and monitor their own personal goals related to independent reading.
3. Programs allow sufficient class time for independent reading while ensuring productive use of this class time.
4. Programs facilitate risk-free opportunities for struggling students to partner with competent readers who will help them follow the text and join in the reading.

In their efforts to promote independent recreational reading, it is wise for teachers to monitor their school library holdings as well as their classroom library collections on a regular basis. In addition to literary texts, do these collections include a broad range of media texts and informational texts? Boys often prefer practical "how to" informational texts over novels or books of poetry. Teachers can leverage their school-based literacy project as an opportunity to intensify the promotion of reading among boys. They can also challenge students who claim not to enjoy reading to identify topics of personal interest: computers, horses, fashion, sports cars, rock stars, and so on. They can expose these students to a wide range of reading materials that will tap into their interests. These materials include books, magazines, websites, comic strips, video game instructions, zines, and so on. Librarians can provide invaluable help in matching reluctant readers with texts that will help motivate them to read.

What else can teachers do to increase their students' independent reading for enjoyment? In some collaborative literacy projects, teachers schedule in-class book talks that showcase diverse voices and perspectives. Students, teachers, authors, and community members are invited to read samples of their favorite texts. Afterwards, they engage in a question-and-answer session with the audience. The implicit message that book talks communicate is that frequent, independent reading enriches one's life and presents a viable alternative to television and other forms of mass entertainment.

As another well-established strategy, teachers can read selected texts aloud to students. As they read, teachers model fluency, enthusiasm, and expressiveness. They also model their personal responses to a variety of literary forms, including expository or informational texts in addition to narrative texts. *Voices of Readers: How We Come to Love Books* (G. Robert Carlson and Ann Sherill, 1988) is based on extensive interviews with hundreds of adult readers. This professional book stresses how important it is for teachers to read aloud to students:

> An important pleasure-filled school memory is that of the teacher's reading aloud. For many it seems to be the teacher's most fondly remembered experience of school years. (p. 16)

> The association of literature and the human voice has a powerful influence on a young person's interest in reading. Over and over the protocols indicate how pleasurable the respondents found the teacher's reading to be. (pp. 45-46)

Given heightened media attention to accountability issues and to school ratings based on standardized test scores, it is understandable that teachers can sometimes lose sight of their core values as educators. Undeniably, increased reading is a major stimulus for vocabulary growth and for enhanced academic performance. However, we must not overlook the fact that the main benefit that students will derive from this particular literacy goal will be a life enriched by reading.

In helping students set and monitor personal goals related to independent reading, teachers must decide whether a target such as reading a book a month independently might be appropriate for their school. Obviously, many students will read beyond the minimum targets. What should those minimum targets be? Literacy coaches explore questions such as these as they work alongside teachers to coordinate efforts to increase students' recreational reading.

Reading Response Options

In working together to increase students' independent reading, teachers should first agree to collectively slay the dragon known as the traditional book report. Extensive reading for enjoyment is impeded by tasks that demand detailed analysis. Thus, many literacy projects focus on eliciting students' personal or

The implicit message that book talks communicate is that frequent, independent reading enriches one's life and presents a viable alternative to television and other forms of mass entertainment.

Extensive reading for enjoyment is impeded by tasks that demand detailed analysis.

emotional reactions to texts. These reactions are often expressed in journal entries or brief book talks in response to prompts such as the following:

- What part of the text did you enjoy most/least?
- What place(s) did the text's setting remind you of?
- What characters did you like best? Why?
- What part of the text really grabbed your interest? Why?
- What other texts that you've read are like this one?
- Would you recommend this text to someone else? Who? Why?
- Would you read another text by this author?
- What did the text help you to understand or to learn?
- Which part of the text are you not sure about?

Some school-based literacy projects ask students to select a response option that includes an opportunity to write, to dramatize, or to create a visual representation such as a poster or a book jacket. *Language Arts Idea Bank* (Foster, 2003) suggests many different response options. Students keep a separate folder in which to store their reading goals, lists of texts they've read, the dates they started and finished the texts, and their work samples. Literacy coaches can help teachers decide which response options and management strategies related to the school's recreational reading program they would like to incorporate.

Timed Reading Records

Teachers must set aside adequate class time for independent reading, but this time must be used productively. Teachers report that free-reading during class time is often wasted. One solution is to have students complete reading records during timed reading periods. Teachers who use reading record forms report that students' reading rates improve as a result. These teachers give students a separate form for each book they read and they store the records in a folder. Here is a recommended procedure for using a reading record form:

1. Before the reading period begins, students record the page on which they will begin their reading. They may use estimates such as "top of page 30," "middle of page 59," or "bottom of page 186."
2. The teacher uses a timer for a set reading period, say, 20 minutes. Exact timing is critical. When the timer buzzes, students stop reading and move on to Step 3.
3. Immediately following the reading period, teachers ask students to record the page on which they stopped reading. Students also record the date, calculate the number of pages they read, and add a brief comment, summary, or prediction, as shown in the form on the next page.

(A blank version of this form for classroom use appears in the Appendices at the back of this book.)

Not only do literacy coaches help colleagues implement methods to ensure productive student use of independent reading time, but they also invite feedback from teachers about the effectiveness of the reading time allotment. If large numbers of students are not reading enthusiastically, coaches should engage colleagues in a frank discussion about the problem. Sometimes, reminding teachers to model their own reading during the assigned reading time can help motivate students to read.

Independent Reading Record

Name: Kim Tan

Title of text: Tom Sawyer

Author: Mark Twain

Date	Start Page	Finish Page	Pages Read	Comment, Summary, or Prediction
Oct. 5	15 (top)	20 (middle)	$4\frac{1}{2}$	The part about Tom giving medicine to the cat is funny. I wonder if something like this could happen in real life.

Support for Struggling Readers

Schools can employ a variety of read-along methods to support struggling readers. One method is to use recorded readings or audio books. It is critical that students follow the printed text during the reading. In addition, volunteer readers or reading buddies can read a text orally with students who find reading difficult. Volunteers and reading buddies invite students to chime in or signal their readiness to read a part of the text on their own. Literacy coaches can remind their colleagues to try various means to engage struggling or reluctant readers in independent reading programs.

All the instructional strategies outlined above have a positive effect on collaborative efforts to promote frequent reading. To decide whether frequent independent reading would be a worthwhile literacy goal for their school, teachers might use a reading profile similar to the one presented on page 00 of Chapter 4. The key questions to explore are:

- How much reading are our students completing?
- How can we work together to motivate students to read more frequently?
- How creative can we be in enticing students to read more and to read widely in terms of genres and text forms?

Coordinating Instruction in Reading Comprehension Strategies

Research by literacy experts such as David Booth and Larry Swartz (*Literacy Techniques*, 2004) has clearly established that readers who can identify the strategies they use before, during, and after their first reading of an unfamiliar text improve their comprehension of that text. Many collaborative literacy projects—similar to the one described in Chapter 4—focus on bolstering students' conscious, independent use of reading comprehension strategies.

To determine whether a reading strategies focus would be an appropriate collaborative literacy goal for their school, teachers could try a simple test with their students. Using a short, unfamiliar text in any subject area, teachers challenge students to write down any strategies that they used before, during, and after their reading. To introduce the activity, teachers discuss with students the meaning and function of the term "strategy" in general: a way of thinking, an approach to solving a problem, a means of completing a task. After they have read the text, students fill out a form such as the one below.

My Reading Strategies

Name: _____   Date: _____

Title of text: _____

Author of text:_____

1. Strategies I used before reading the text:

_____

_____

_____

2. Strategies I used as I read the text:

_____

_____

_____

3. Strategies I used after reading the text:

_____

_____

_____

If significant numbers of students cannot identify reasonable strategies, then a focus on improved use of reading comprehension strategies would constitute a suitable collaborative literacy goal.

The professional development related to implementing the goal should recommend that teachers use similar language to describe strategies that proficient readers use before, during, and after they first read an unfamiliar text. Transitions among grades and subject areas and transfer of learning are fostered when students hear and see familiar, standard terminology to describe reading strategies.

The following chart presents some reading strategies explored in depth in professional literature such as *New Directions in Reading Instruction* (Hinson, 2000), *Literacy Techniques* (Booth, Second Edition, 2004*), Lessons in Comprehension: Explicit Instruction in the Reading Workshop* (Serafini, 2004), and *What Good Readers Do: Seven Steps to Better Reading* (Foster, 2005). If they wish, students

Transitions among grades and subject areas and transfer of learning are fostered when students hear and see familiar, standard terminology to describe reading strategies.

and teachers can work together to reproduce poster-size versions of this chart to display in their classrooms. They could also encourage students to make bookmarks listing some of these strategies as memory cues.

READING COMPREHENSION STRATEGIES

Before Reading	During Reading	After Reading
Setting a purpose for reading	Chunking the text into meaningful units	Checking and revising earlier predictions
Previewing a text's title, illustrations, and photo captions	Making predictions about characters, events, facts, or ideas in the text	Answering questions posed during reading
Identifying the text form (short story, poem, cartoon, recount, information report, procedural text, photo essay, and so on)	Visualizing	Rereading parts of the text to refine interpretations or conclusions, or to check answers selected on a reading test.
Predicting what the text will be about	Asking questions about the text	Retelling
Recalling other texts written by the same author	Making personal connections to the text	Summarizing the main ideas in the text
Scanning the text for familiar and unfamiliar vocabulary	Checking or rereading something that does not make sense (monitoring comprehension)	
Activating prior knowledge of the topic	Paying close attention to the final chunk of text (it often emphasizes a point, presents a surprising twist, or shows a character's final reaction)	
Building background knowledge of the topic		
Asking questions about what content might be included in the text		

Every day, teachers can encourage students at all grade levels to think about and apply the reading comprehension strategies that work best for them in the various curricular areas. At regular intervals, students can complete a reading strategies organizer, such as the one on the following page, to help them identify and label the strategies they employed successfully before, during, and after reading an unfamiliar text. (A blank version of this graphic organizer for classroom use appears in the Appendices at the back of this book.)

To track students' progress during a reading-focused collaborative literacy project, teachers agree to have students complete at least two reading strategy organizers throughout the year. Teachers are free to assign these organizers more often if they think their students would benefit from more frequent opportunities to reflect on their use of reading strategies. Some teachers record and note progress in terms of the number of different strategies that students can use and identify appropriately. In the example above, the student has identified five strategies:

1. I looked at the picture.—activating prior knowledge
2. I thought about hockey.—building background knowledge
3. I pictured the story.—visualizing
4. I pretended to be the boy.—connecting to personal experience
5. I checked words I wasn't sure of.—monitoring comprehension

Literacy coaches can remind their colleagues that these reading organizers represent a source of valuable assessment data pertaining to the collaborative literacy project.

Emphasizing Higher-Level Thinking Skills

In the early stages of planning and implementing a reading-focused literacy project, participants should agree to honour two essential ground rules:

1. Teachers must identify explicitly the specific skills or outcomes that students are expected to demonstrate or achieve when they read a particular text.
2. Questions posed about particular texts should include higher-level thinking skills if and when it is appropriate to include higher-order thinking.

Literacy coaches play an important role in helping colleagues develop a shared taxonomy of thinking skills related to reading. Three levels of thinking typify the questions that students ask and answer about the texts they read:

Literal Thinking/Questioning—To answer a literal question, the reader must locate information that is stated directly in the text.

Inferential Thinking/Questioning—To answer an inferential question, the reader must make an inference by combining background knowledge with details provided in the text. (This is sometimes called "reading between the lines.") To answer an inferential question, a reader can also combine various details provided in the text to make an interpretation or form a conclusion.

Evaluative Thinking/Questioning—To answer an evaluative question, the reader must judge whether the text or a particular text feature is worthwhile, realistic, effective, or true. Answering an evaluative question involves identifying the author's point of view and assessing whether that point of view is valid, in other words, supported by credible evidence provided in the text.

The following poem was written by a Grade 5 student. Note how the questions posed about the poem illustrate the three levels of thinking.

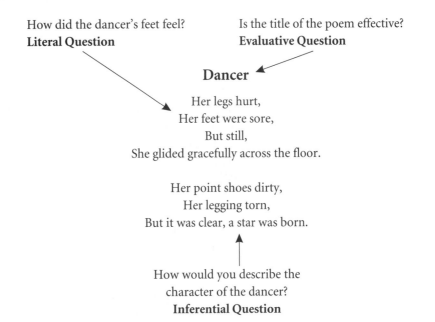

How did the dancer's feet feel?
Literal Question

Is the title of the poem effective?
Evaluative Question

Dancer

Her legs hurt,
Her feet were sore,
But still,
She glided gracefully across the floor.

Her point shoes dirty,
Her legging torn,
But it was clear, a star was born.

How would you describe the character of the dancer?
Inferential Question

Questions that reflect different levels of thinking are largely determined by the text itself. For example, how-to manuals, instruction sheets, cookbooks, and science lab reports generally present information literally. Literature, on the other hand, often communicates ideas indirectly and implicitly and therefore requires inferential thinking on the part of a reader. Opinion pieces, letters to the editor, advertisements, and public service announcements express a particular point of view and tend to omit alternative perspectives. These text forms require evaluative thinking on the part of the reader.

Below is a sample list of frequently-asked questions labeled *L* for literal, *I* for inferential, and/or *E* for evaluative. Note that the same question can demand a different level of thinking depending upon how information is provided in the text. For example, some texts require that the reader infer the author's purpose, while other texts state the author's purpose directly.

Purpose/Topic/Audience

What is the author's topic? (L)
What is the author's purpose in writing? (L, I)
What main ideas does the author express? (L, I)
What is the author's attitude toward the topic? (I)
Who is the author's audience? (L, I)
Is the author's topic interesting? (E)
Is the author's purpose worthwhile? (E)
Do you agree with the main ideas expressed by the author? (E)
Do you agree with the author's attitude toward the topic? (E)
Does the author adequately support his or her point of view? (E)

Text Structure

What title has the author chosen for the text? (L)
How has the author structured the text? (L, I)
How does the author create interest in the introduction? (I)
How does the author create interest in the conclusion? (I)
Is the title effective? (E)
Is the text structure effective? (E)
Is the introduction effective? (E)
Is the conclusion effective? (E)

Voice

What does the word _____ mean? (L, I)
What important details related to the topic does the author include?
   (L, I, E)
What comparisons or figures of speech does the author include? (L)
What ideas are suggested by the comparisons and figures of
   speech? (I)
Are the author's word choices effective? (E)
Are the author's comparisons and figures of speech effective? (E)
Are the author's comparisons and figures of speech original? (E)

Literary Techniques

What is the setting of the story? (L)
What is the main character like? (I)
How does the main character develop or change as the story unfolds? (I)
What is the central conflict in the story? (I)
What is the climax of the story? (I)
Which of the following literary techniques does the author employ:
   atmosphere, suspense, irony, figurative language? (I)
Does each character speak and behave appropriately and consistently? (E)
Are the characters plausible? (E)
How effectively does the author use literary techniques such as
   atmosphere, suspense, irony, and figurative language? (E)

In coordinating practice related to the higher-level thinking skills involved in reading, teachers need to work together to adopt or develop a taxonomy similar to the one presented on the previous page. Groups can make the taxonomy their own by suggesting additions, deletions, and modifications. As students read texts across grades and subject areas, teachers reflect on the kinds of questions that each text requires—literal, inferential, or evaluative. Where appropriate on a case-by-case basis, they pose higher-level thinking questions to students.

Many literacy projects challenge students to *pose* rather than respond to questions. This provides a valuable exercise in higher-order thinking as students themselves devise prompts such as: "What important questions does this text raise?" By encouraging students to construct their own questions about a text, teachers challenge students to recognize questions that demand higher-level thinking and close reading. At the same time, teachers do not overlook the importance and validity of personal and emotional responses to texts, as described in the first section of this chapter.

Differentiated Instruction

Higher-level thinking skills offer a natural opportunity for differentiated instruction. For example, if students are asked to judge whether a character behaves appropriately in dealing with a conflict, they can choose one of several response options:

- They might dramatize the conflict.
- They could create a visual representation of the conflict.
- They could write a monologue to explore the character's inner experiences.

Literacy coaches can reinforce the important realization that higher-level thinking can be expressed through action and visual representations as well as through words.

To document students' progress, many teachers create reading tests based on texts appropriate to the subject area they are teaching. Tests should include key questions suggested by the text with an emphasis on questions requiring higher-level thinking skills, if and when such questions suit the text. By administering at least two tests featuring texts of similar levels of difficulty, teachers can assess students' progress throughout the literacy project. Literacy coaches remind colleagues that parallel test results provide valuable assessment data related to students' reading skills.

Emphasizing Close Reading of Texts

Many literacy experts have articulated the challenge of encouraging students to pay close attention to textual details. Details that support a main idea offer clues to the author's purpose and message, both explicit and implicit. Therefore, collaborative literacy projects often focus on close reading of a text. What can we do collaboratively so that students will attend more carefully to the details in texts?

Professional literature such as *New Directions in Reading Instruction* (Hinson, 2000) offers effective instructional strategies related to close reading of texts. At the beginning of a collaborative literacy project, teachers should meet several

Higher-level thinking skills offer a natural opportunity for differentiated instruction.

times to share and consolidate their learning about close-reading strategies. Throughout the project, they need to plan lessons that embed close-reading strategies such as the ones outlined below. During team meetings, literacy coaches encourage the sharing of graphic organizers and other close-reading instructional material that colleagues have either collected or created together. (Teachers often organize their shared instructional material in a three-ring binder.) The following approaches can be easily incorporated into reading tasks across grades and subject areas.

Encouraging Use of Graphic Organizers

Visual learners especially benefit from working with graphic organizers that support close reading of a text. Webs such as the one below are an excellent tool for recording the main topic (in the centre of the web), subtopics, and important details in a piece of informational or descriptive text.

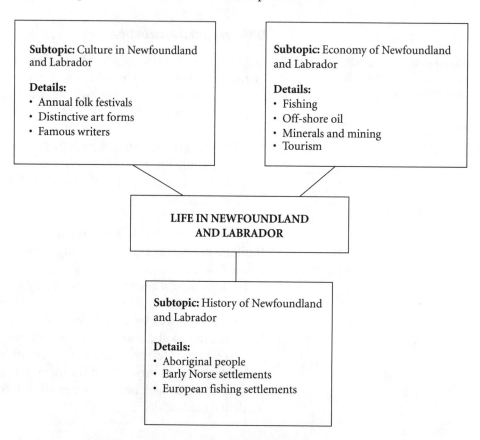

When closely reading texts organized according to a sequence pattern—for example, history texts or procedural texts—students can make a timeline to record important details, as shown below.

IMPORTANT EVENTS IN THE SEVEN YEARS WAR IN EUROPE

1. Prussians capture Savoy	2. Prussians defeat French at Rothback	3. Prussians defeat Austrians at Leuthen	4. Russians invade Prussia	5. Russians and Swedes withdraw from war
1756	1757	1757	1759	1762

Sequencing activities designed to foster close reading of a text can be enjoyable, especially for kinesthetic learners. For example, teachers can give students a passage to read, along with an envelope containing cut-up sections of the same text. Their task is to assemble the chunks of texts in order, an activity that demands close attention to textual detail. Short poems and brief newspaper articles lend themselves as well to this type of sequencing activity.

To help students pay close attention to textual details related to the conflict, climax, and resolution in a narrative text, teachers can distribute a chart such as the one below for students to fill in. (A Grade 5 student completed this chart. A blank version of the chart for classroom use appears in the Appendices at the back of this book.)

Narrative Elements Chart

Name: _____ Title: "The House on the Hill" _____

SOMEBODY (central character)	Marsha, a ten-year-old girl
SOMEWHERE (setting)	late on a dark night on a deserted city street
WANTED (character's goal)	Marsha wanted to get home safely after collecting Halloween candy.
BUT (conflict)	Marsha encountered scary noises and what looked like a headless figure.
SO (climax)	Marsha's brother zoomed up on a bike and pulled a cloth off the head of the friend who had tricked Marsha.
THEN (character's reaction)	Marsha realized how much she appreciated her brother's help.
AND IT ALL GOES TO SHOW THAT… (theme)	We appreciate friends and family most when we are in trouble.

Other ideas for close-reading activities are offered in *What Good Readers Do: Seven Steps to Better Reading* (Foster, 2005). Teachers who have teamed up to coordinate practice related to close reading of a text typically employ parallel reading tests at the beginning and at the end of their literacy project. These teachers work together to develop a taxonomy (similar to that in the previous section) to develop test questions appropriate to a selected text. Teachers often base their reading tests on texts of similar length and difficulty level so that they can track student progress. On the other hand, teachers also occasionally develop one reading test to use both at the beginning and at the end of the project to track progress in students' reading comprehension.

Culminating Tasks and Extension Activities

Literacy projects focused on students' reading of a text or a collection of texts often conclude with a culminating task or an extension activity—an assignment that requires them to *do* something with the text or texts. For example, students might engage in the activities listed on the following page.

- write a brief report or journal entry about the text(s)
- perform the text as a skit, interview, or Readers' Theatre
- create a visual representation of the text: a PowerPoint presentation, a poster, a photo essay, and so on

Culminating tasks conclude a unit of work. Extension activities, on the other hand, integrate reading with one or more of the other language arts: writing, speaking, listening, viewing, and representing. Effective extension activities encourage careful and thoughtful reading of the text. Sometimes teachers differentiate instruction by allowing a wide range of options for extension activities to accommodate diverse learning styles: hands-on, musical, visual-spatial, artistic, and so on.

Collaborative literacy projects may feature culminating tasks or text extension activities that emphasize reading comprehension. At the beginning of the project, colleagues share and review possible ideas for culminating tasks and extension activities. Throughout the project, they plan tasks or activities that improve students' reading ability.

Once again, literacy coaches encourage colleagues to share ideas and instructional resources collected or created for culminating tasks or extension activities. Teachers share materials and discuss their effectiveness at their regularly scheduled literacy team meetings. Several ideas for extension activities appear below.

Oral Interpretation of a Text

Students prepare and present an oral interpretation or Readers' Theatre version of a short text or an excerpt from a longer text. Teachers challenge them to meet the following criteria in their oral presentation:

- The oral interpretation clearly builds to a climax or focal point.
- The oral interpretation demonstrates appropriate tone and volume and appropriate variation in speaking quickly or slowly, loudly or softly.
- The oral interpretation demonstrates thoughtful pacing—students' rate of reading or speaking increases or decreases effectively and appropriately.
- The oral interpretation respects punctuation cues: pauses at commas, stops at periods, and appropriate intonation for question marks and exclamation points.

Teachers can assess students' progress in meeting criteria such as those above by having students complete two or more oral interpretations of a text throughout the school year. Formal oral interpretation activities offer an excellent alternative to round-robin reading because less proficient readers may practice as much as they like to ensure a confident presentation. Oral reading practice and stopping to think about climax, volume, pace, and punctuation cues demand close reading of a text and therefore enhanced reading comprehension.

In collaborative literacy projects, teachers typically require students to complete at least two oral interpretation tasks. Teachers observe and make notes about students' levels of improvement according to criteria such as those listed above. They can use or adapt the rubric on the following page to assess each student's oral interpretation of a text.

A Rubric for Oral Interpretation of Literature

	Level 1 **Needs Extra Support**	Level 2 **Novice**	Level 3 **Competent**	Level 4 **Proficient**
Preparation	Demonstrates little preparation of oral interpretation	Demonstrates limited preparation of oral Interpretation	Demonstrates considerable preparation of oral interpretation	Demonstrates thoughtful preparation of oral interpretation
Punctuation Cues	Disregards punctuation cues	Intreprets a few punctuation cues	Interprets most punctuation cues	Interprets all punctuation cues
Timing and Pacing	Seldom uses timing and pacing for appropriate emphasis	Sometimes uses timing and pacing for appropriate emphasis	Usually uses timing and pacing for appropriate emphasis	Consistently uses timing and pacing for appropriate emphasis
Volume	Seldom uses appropriate volume and appropriate variation in volume	Sometimes uses appropriate volume and appropriate variation in volume	Usually uses appropriate volume and appropriate variation in volume	Consistently uses appropriate volume and appropriate variation in volume
Emphasis	Does not succeed in building to a focal point	Hints at a focal point	Indicates a focal point and builds to a focal point	Clearly indicates a focal point and builds to a focal point

Visual Representations of a Text

By means of carefully crafted assignments, teachers can invite students to complete visual representation tasks to encourage close, thoughtful reading of a text. Visual representation assignments include tasks such as:

- sketching or drawing scenes from the text
- creating a cartoon or comic strip version of the text
- preparing a book jacket or movie poster for the text
- drawing a timeline or map for the text
- creating a game or crossword puzzle based on the text

By challenging students to explain how their visual representation emphasizes important textual details, teachers encourage close reading of the text. As part of the assignment, teachers inform students that they must provide a written or oral explanation of how their visual representation accentuates textual details. Teachers also gauge students' ability to evaluate the visual representation itself.

In collaborative literacy projects, teachers typically design at least two parallel visual representation tasks. As part of their assessment plan, teachers note the level of improvement in students' ability to identify how their representation highlights critical details in the text.

Written Extensions of a Text

Students often employ someone else's text to inspire their own writing. Written extension activities include options such as:

- writing a brief position paper or report
- preparing an interview with a character in the text
- writing a diary entry or a monologue told from a character's point of view
- rewriting the text in a different form, for example, writing a dramatic script for a short story
- writing a prequel or sequel to the text
- writing about memories evoked by the text
- writing an obituary for a character in the text, or
- writing a letter to a friend to express a personal reaction to a text

For successful completion, each of these activities demands close, thoughtful reading of the text.

As part of their assessment of writing assignments that follow reading of selected texts, teachers should include criteria related to textual detail. Rubrics may include criteria such as those below to emphasize close reading of a text.

Level 1 Needs Extra Support	Level 2 Novice	Level 3 Competent	Level 4 Proficient
The writing rarely refers to specific details from the source text.	The writing sometimes refers to specific details from the source text.	The writing regularly refers to specific details from the source text.	The writing extensively refers to specific details from the source text.

By employing these criteria at least twice during the school year, teachers observe and make notes on students' progress in attending to textual details.

For all the literacy project options described in this chapter, a literacy coach continually searches for relevant professional development material. This material includes journal articles, trade books, textbooks, Internet articles, DVDs, webcasts, and workshops related to the project goal that the team has selected. The literacy coach encourages colleagues to search for material as well to share and discuss at team meetings.

Checklist for Literacy Coaches and Administrators

Literacy coaches and school administrators may use this checklist to ensure they have met the following criteria in exploring and refining a collaborative literacy project related to best practice in reading instruction:

☐ We have helped colleagues explore several options before choosing a focus for our collaborative reading project.

☐ We have encouraged colleagues to consider extensive independent reading as a project priority.

☐ We have encouraged colleagues to consider reading strategies as a project priority.

☐ We have encouraged colleagues to consider higher-level thinking skills as a project priority.

☐ We have encouraged colleagues to consider close reading of texts as a project priority.

☐ We have encouraged colleagues to consider emphasis on reading comprehension in culminating tasks and extension activities as a project priority.

☐ We have encouraged colleagues to identify a specific focus for our collaborative reading project.

☐ We have helped colleagues develop an appropriate assessment strategy for our collaborative reading project.

☐ We have provided opportunities for colleagues to meet to share and discuss instructional materials they have collected and/or created for use in our collaborative reading project.

6

Collaborative Projects in Writing Instruction

Selecting a Best-Practice Goal

Chapter 5 explored how teachers and literacy coaches can work together to review professional literature on best practice in reading instruction as a springboard to planning a collaborative reading project for their school. This chapter discusses how a similar review can help a school's staff select a writing focus for their project. Successful collaborative writing projects focus on one of the following best-practice goals:

1. Improve students' writing ability by emphasizing writing to learn as well as writing to communicate
2. Improve students' writing ability by coordinating instruction in writing strategies
3. Improve students' writing ability by emphasizing voice in writing and qualities that make acceptable writing extraordinary
4. Improve students' writing ability through coordinated assessment practice
5. Improve students' writing ability by developing exemplar lessons

Chapter 6 will look at collaborative approaches to meeting each of these goals. As in Chapter 5, this chapter will sidestep detailed discussion of specific organizational methods used by individual teachers to teach writing outcomes. Some teachers employ a workshop approach involving differentiated writing tasks and an emphasis on mini-lessons and conferences. They might structure their lessons to teach the six traits of writing (ideas, organization, voice, word choice, fluency, and conventions). Other teachers focus their instruction on a particular writing form, such as editorials, information reports, or short stories. Some teachers use composition textbooks in their classrooms. Others do not. Literacy coaches can remind teachers that despite differences in organizational methods, everyone can pursue the same shared goal of helping their students become better writers.

Emphasizing Writing to Learn

Teachers concerned about their students' writing ability often come to the realization that as a result of a crowded curriculum, students may simply not be writing enough. Therefore, teachers in some schools take steps to survey the amount of composition that students are doing in the course of a day or a week. If they conclude that the amount is insufficient, they might choose to coordinate their efforts to increase the amount of student writing by placing an emphasis on *writing to learn* rather than writing to communicate.

We tend to view writing primarily as a communication tool. While undeniably valid, this viewpoint is somewhat narrow. Teachers and students often do not realize that writing is an important way to explore ideas, to think, and to learn content. For example, suppose that students are studying osmosis in science. Their teachers have decided to coordinate writing instruction by focusing on writing to learn. They give students opportunities to write about their current understanding of osmosis. In their writing, students set goals related to what they would like to find out about this scientific phenomenon. Through research, writing, and rewriting, they consolidate their understanding of the topic as they uncover gaps in their knowledge and strive to fill those gaps. Writing to learn is a powerful tool. It helps students direct their own learning based on what they already know about a topic as well as what they would like to discover in order to satisfy their curiosity.

> Writing to learn is a powerful tool. It helps students direct their own learning based on what they already know about a topic as well as what they would like to discover in order to satisfy their curiosity.

Using Learning Logs as a Writing-to-Learn Tool

When teachers decide to focus on writing to learn as a collaborative goal, they often agree to schedule regular opportunities for students to complete learning log activities. They may set a minimum target, for example, one learning log entry per day. Since composition often features both words and images, they adopt a broad conceptualization of writing as work that incorporates visual representations, mathematical problems, media components, and so on. Together, colleagues brainstorm a list of writing response options for students' learning log entries, for example:

- Comments, questions, and/or predictions about a topic of interest
- Connections to other learning and to personal experience
- Current understandings related to a topic or concept
- Examples of new learning
- Judgments or arguments related to a topic
- Observations about people, objects, or events
- Doubts about a position or a point of view
- Evidence of changing one's opinion about a topic
- Goals and plans related to exploration of a topic
- Graphic organizers or diagrams to represent ideas or processes
- Strategies designed to help complete a task

Additionally, writing to learn in language arts may take the form of written personal responses to literature. Prompts included in the section titled "Reading Response Options" in Chapter 5 encourage this type of exploratory writing (see page 55).

Throughout the school year, teachers assess the benefits of regularly scheduled writing-to-learn activities. As a result of these activities, do students do better when tested on content? Does more writing practice lead to improved formal writing skills over time? Teachers can assess students' learning log entries to check for improved fluency; greater attention to details presented in a lesson, reading, or media text; and evidence of exploratory thinking and risk-taking. *Response Journals Revisited* (Parsons, 2001) presents practical, motivational writing-to-learn options that many teachers find helpful.

Literacy coaches arrange meetings with colleagues to discuss and solidify the writing response options they would like to implement. Colleagues also share any instructional material they have already gathered or developed to encourage writing to learn. Coaches should encourage teachers to collect exemplars of student work related to the writing-to-learn goal. These exemplars represent valuable teaching resources because teachers can show students the thinking and learning that emerged as a result of various writing-to-learn activities. (A later section of this chapter will discuss guidelines for collecting exemplars.)

Assessing Writing-to-Learn Projects

To facilitate assessment of writing-to-learn projects, colleagues can work together to develop a rubric to track students' progress. The rubric could feature criteria such as the following:

Criteria	Level 1 Needs Extra Support	Level 2 Novice	Level 3 Competent	Level 4 Proficient
Completion	Few required learning log entries completed	Some required learning log entries completed	Most required learning log entries completed	All required learning log entries completed
Level of Detail	Little detail is presented in learning log entries	Limited detail is presented in learning log entries	Adequate detail is presented in learning log entries	Extensive detail is presented in learning log entries
Variety of Response Options	No variety in response options is demonstrated in learning log entries	Limited variety in response options is demonstrated in learning log entries	Adequate variety in response options is demonstrated in learning log entries	Extensive variety in response options is demonstrated in learning log entries

Coordinating Instruction in Writing Strategies

Research summarized by George Hillocks (1986, 1995) strongly indicates that students who can identify the strategies they use before, during, and after they write a first draft meet learning outcomes more successfully than students who cannot. Therefore, many collaborative literacy projects focus on reinforcing students' use of writing strategies across grades and subject areas.

Recall that evidence of students' inability to identify reading strategies can point teachers toward a collaborative literacy project focused on reading instruction. Similarly, evidence of students' inability to identify pre-writing, drafting, and revision strategies may point a literacy team toward a school-based collaborative writing project. To gain quick feedback on students' knowledge and use of writing strategies, teachers may ask students to fill out a survey such as the one on the following page. How capably can students identify the writing strategies they use as they complete a writing assignment?

Writing Strategies Self-Assessment Chart

Name: _____

Date: _____

Title of Composition: _____

1. Strategies I used before writing the first draft: _____

_____

_____

_____

_____

_____

_____

_____

2. Strategies I used as I wrote the first draft—especially when I got stuck: _____

_____

_____

_____

_____

_____

_____

_____

3. Strategies I used after I wrote the first draft: _____

_____

_____

_____

_____

_____

_____

_____

Professional development related to the collaborative literacy goal must support teachers in developing a common language to describe writing strategies that students can use before, during, and after they compose a first draft. The following chart presents an adapted overview of the writing strategies featured in *Seven Steps to Successful Writing* (Foster, 2004). Note that advising students to read over their first drafts to identify elements that need improvement is too general to be helpful. Students will revise their writing more successfully if they check against *specific criteria* (see the chart below).

Note also the critical importance of advising students to spend sufficient time on pre-writing planning. Often writer's block results from insufficient planning.

HELPFUL STRATEGIES FOR BEFORE, DURING, AND AFTER WRITING

Before Writing (first draft)	During Writing (first draft)	After Writing (first draft)
Think about and make notes on writing variables such as role, audience, format, topic, purpose, and voice.	Explain to someone what you are trying to write.	Read your writing aloud to a partner and ask for feedback. Is your writing clear?
Choose a pre-writing strategy that fits the text form, e.g., direct observation when writing a descriptive paragraph; a story map when writing a narrative; a web or concept map when writing an expository piece; a Venn diagram when writing a piece featuring comparison/contrast.	Begin with the second paragraph rather than drafting your introductory paragraph; return to the introduction after you have completed your first draft.	Make revisions according to specific criteria, e.g., check for features such as precise vocabulary; effective transitions; details that match your purpose and audience; varied sentence types; varied sentence lengths; effective leads (beginnings) and endings (conclusions).
	If you cannot think of an appropriate word or phrase, leave a blank and come back to it later. Mark an "S" over words if you are unsure of their spelling; consult a dictionary for correct spellings and make corrections later.	Edit/proofread your draft using standard proofreading symbols; check for correct use of grammar, punctuation, and syntax.
	Write on every second line of a lined sheet of paper so that you can easily make corrections as you write.	

To support students as they complete writing tasks in all grades and subject areas, teachers can model and label the strategies they use in their own writing.

To support students as they complete writing tasks in all grades and subject areas, teachers can model and label the strategies they use in their own writing. They can use think-alouds to describe their thought processes and the decisions they make in the various stages of the writing process: planning (pre-writing), drafting, rethinking and revising, reflecting, editing, and publishing. Whenever an opportunity arises, teachers should model their own use of writing strategies. After sufficient modeling, students can begin to identify the strategies that work best for them in completing specific writing tasks. Just as for reading strategies, it is beneficial for students to chart their use of writing strategies at regular intervals. This enables teachers to assess progress in students' ability to identify, label, and apply a variety of strategies.

Below is an example of a Grade 6 student's writing chart. (A blank version of this graphic organizer for classroom use appears in the Appendices at the back of this book.)

Understanding Myself as a Writer

Name: _____   Date: _____ May 30 _____

Writing Assignment: _ newspaper article _____

Strategies I used before drafting:

I first used a graphic organizer and RAFTS (review of role, audience, format, topic, and strong verb or purpose for writing task).

Strategies I used during drafting:

Focusing on the topic. No using dull words and listing words. Form a picture in the reader's mind.

Strategies I used after drafting:

Going over spelling, tense and sentence structure. Replacing ordinary words with more descriptive words. Read it over. Punctuate.

Literacy coaches are responsible for determining the depth of teachers' knowledge of the "before/during/after" writing process model presented in this section. In my experience, teachers vary greatly in their familiarity with this model. If teachers need some coaching in using the model, a best-practice workshop dedicated to the writing process would be helpful. In the workshop, teachers can plan activities to help students identify and use strategies before, during, and after writing a draft in a particular content area.

Emphasizing Voice and Making Acceptable Writing Extraordinary

In selecting a collaborative literacy goal, some schools decide to focus on adding value to acceptable student writing. Teachers' assessment of writing often indicates that many students achieve acceptable ratings but few excel. Therefore, schools sometimes choose to concentrate on instructional strategies to help students move from acceptable to extraordinary writing. To nudge students toward excellence in writing, collaborative projects often emphasize voice. In addition, these projects often stress how to compose beginnings and endings that command attention.

Writing with a Strong Voice

The voice in which fiction and non-fiction are written reveals the personality, attitudes, feelings, and point of view of the writer. A strong voice can be either formal or informal, serious or humorous, lively or pedestrian. Voice varies to suit the text form the writer has chosen, as well as the writer's purpose and audience. Writers convey voice through tone, word choice, word order, sentence structure, and details included in the text. Writing experts emphasize three important characteristics of voice:

> Voice varies to suit the text form the writer has chosen, as well as the writer's purpose and audience.

- Honesty and evidence of caring about one's writing rather than wooden and contrived writing
- Originality in word choice, details, and figures of speech rather than humdrum details and clichés
- Showing rather than telling

Teachers can help students develop a strong voice in their writing by encouraging them to reflect on key questions such as:

1. How can I convey my honest feelings most clearly?
2. What details might I include to make my writing as strong as possible?
3. Where would my writing benefit from more showing and less telling?
4. What words might I change to add uniqueness to my expression?
5. How I can I change figures of speech to add originality and avoid clichés?

One effective instructional approach is to display and discuss examples of writing that exhibits a strong voice. Published writing can exemplify both formal and informal voice, depending on the author's purpose and audience.

Even more powerful are student exemplars. After examining some exemplars together, teachers can challenge students to revise a composition by adding original details, by injecting color and creativity into word choice and figures of speech, and by showing rather than telling. Research by George Hillocks in *Research on Written Composition: New Directions for Teaching* (1986) shows clearly that revising one's work according to specific criteria such as those listed above leads to improved writing ability.

Improving Introductions and Conclusions

Another method teachers use to show students how to transform ordinary writing into exceptional writing is to strengthen introductions and conclusions. Literacy projects can coordinate instruction in writing across grades and subject areas by focusing on techniques such as the ones illustrated in the charts that appear on pages 79 and 80.

Assessing Quality in Voice, Introductions, and Conclusions

In value-added writing projects, teachers use the same rubric to assess at least two writing samples throughout the year. They note students' progress over time, especially in terms of the number of students who achieve improved rubric ratings. The assessment criteria featured in the rubric on page 81 may prove helpful.

Effective Introductions

Exposition	Narrative
A. Ask a question. • Do you feel inadequate when you speak in public?	**A. Present a brief dialogue that signals tension or conflict.** • "Dad, the water's too high!" My father yelled back, "Quick! Paddle to shore!"
B. State an attention-grabbing fact. • Few people would know how to survive if they became lost or injured in the wilderness.	**B. Plunge the reader into a conflict or a dramatic event.** • Mr. Thorkild was the new neighbour of Sue and Tim Johnson. Late on a moonlit night, Sue and Tim noticed him burying a box in his backyard. Sue inched over to her brother and asked, "I wonder what could be in the box?"
C. State and refute a foolish or incorrect view. • Many people believe that the Internet is just for technical experts or "geeks." Nothing could be further from the truth; everybody can benefit from using the Internet.	**C. Describe a setting with a focus on movement or action related to the story's conflict.** • Over 200 spectators sat in the school gym waiting for the junior boys' team to appear. We hunched at the entrance doors peeking at Mr. Lumbey, our coach, for a signal. Our task—to enter without tripping and to sink a basket on our way to the players' bench. I was completely petrified. As the crowd roared in response to the acrobatic cheerleaders, I convinced myself that if I didn't fall on my face, I'd miss my shot.
D. Use a quotation. • "We are our brother's keeper." Because human beings are at their best when they care for one another, all of us should learn first aid so that we can help in emergencies.	

Effective Conclusions

Exposition	Narrative
A. Answer questions posed in the introduction. • You may feel inadequate when you must speak in public. However, with preparation and practice, you can become a confident public speaker. **B. Make a surprising or powerful final point.** • John Adams lay pinned under his snowmobile for three days. He nearly gave up on being rescued. Without his knowledge of survival techniques, he would have died. His knowledge saved his life. **C. Warn the reader.** • Unless you constantly upgrade your computer skills, you'll be left behind. The best jobs will go to other people and you'll be overlooked for promotions. So don't be a dinosaur—get online today! **D Offer a prediction.** • Now that 40 people in the Belleview community have just graduated from the Red Cross first aid and lifesaving course, someone's life will be saved. That life could be yours.	**A. Present a surprising twist.** • In the story, a boy describes how he and his father are whitewater rafting. Before they begin their adventure, the boy tells his father that the water is too high. The father shrugs off his son's concern. In a few moments, the boy's kayak slams into a huge rock, plunging him into the icy water. Stunned, the boy barely recalls being pulled out of the water. As his father carries him to the car, the boy mumbles, "I told you the water was too high!" **B. Present the character's final reaction.** • In the story, a girl tells about walking home on a dark night. Following a series of frightening experiences, she encounters the most frightening sight of all. A headless creature comes rushing towards her. Her brother zooms up on his bike and pushes the creature over to reveal friends in a hooded costume. The girl realizes how she had previously taken her brother for granted. She tells a friend: "I'm glad my brother was worried about me and came to look out for me!"

Rubric for Assessing Voice, Introductions, and Conclusions

Criteria	Level 1 Needs Extra Support	Level 2 Novice	Level 3 Competent	Level 4 Proficient
Honesty and Caring	Rarely demonstrates honesty and caring about writing	Sometimes demonstrates honesty and caring about writing	Regularly demonstrates honesty and caring about writing	Consistently demonstrates honesty and caring about writing
Diction	Rarely employs unique and appropriate words	Sometimes employs unique and appropriate words	Regularly employs unique and appropriate words	Consistently employs unique and appropriate words
Details and Imagery	Rarely employs unique details and imagery	Sometimes employs unique details and imagery	Regularly employs unique details and imagery	Consistently employs unique details and imagery
Introduction	Introduction is confusing	Introduction is predictable	Introduction creates interest	Introduction commands attention
Conclusion	Conclusion is confusing	Conclusion is predictable	Conclusion creates interest	Conclusion commands attention

Coordinating Writing Assessment Practice

Collaborative literacy projects focused on writing assessment practice explore three critical questions:

1. What qualities do we wish to emphasize in our assessment of writing?
2. How do we know that our grade-level expectations for writing are reasonable?
3. How do we respond effectively to students' writing?

The first question nudges colleagues to reach agreement on descriptions of good writing. Literacy coaches recognize that not all teachers share a common understanding of what constitutes good writing. Therefore, working together to review selected rubrics can be exremely helpful. In group discussions, teachers examine what the rubrics have to say about good writing. Some school-based literacy projects focus on collegial development of rubrics related to specific writing forms such as information articles, poetry, or lab reports. As mentioned in Chapter 4, the creation and sharing of teachers' own instructional material signals the highest level of professional development.

The rubric on page 83 was developed by a group of junior high language arts and social studies teachers for use in assessing expository writing.

In my experience, the second critical question about writing standards and grade-level expectations has led to some of the most powerful professional development I have witnessed in schools. Typically, the question motivates teachers to collect grade-level writing samples or exemplars. Elementary teachers usually begin by gathering samples of their students' narrative writing, possibly but not necessarily timed writing in response to a prompt. Teachers then engage in group marking of selected pieces. Their goal is to collect grade-level exemplars of both acceptable and exceptional writing. Teachers often describe the group assessment and selection of grade-level exemplars as providing the richest professional development they have ever experienced.

Note that literacy coaches and school administrators must ensure that district guidelines are followed when teachers collect exemplars. Parents or guardians must sign a release form to allow their children's work to be used as exemplars. Children's work must remain anonymous, especially if the exemplars are posted to a website. To ensure safety and anonymity, literacy coaches and principals coordinate teachers' collection and photocopying of students' work.

New teachers especially view such collections as extremely helpful in establishing expectations related to excellence in writing. Since student exemplars "show" what rubrics "tell," exemplars serve as a powerful tool in helping colleagues establish clear and unambiguous grade-level expectations.

The third critical question about writing assessment practice leads colleagues toward professional literature describing how a teacher's response can foster student learning. Most teachers would agree that while assessment aligns with accountability, assessment is predominantly about student learning. How can we improve assessment practice so that students will be motivated to improve their writing?

Research summarized by George Hillocks in *Research on Written Composition: New Directions for Teaching* (1986) underscores the negligible value of long written suggestions from teachers in improving student writing. Hillocks' research argues for a selected focus on specific criteria and for positive feedback.

Teachers often describe the group assessment and selection of grade-level exemplars as providing the richest professional development they have ever experienced.

Expository Writing Rubric

	Level 1 Needs Extra Support	Level 2 Novice	Level 3 Competent	Level 4 Proficient
Content	• rarely uses thoughtful and insightful ideas related to the purpose • rarely employs ideas relevant to the topic • offers little evidence of a preview	• sometimes uses thoughtful and insightful ideas related to the purpose • sometimes employs ideas relevant to the topic • offers a partial preview	• regularly uses thoughtful and insightful ideas related to the purpose • sometimes employs ideas relevant to the topic • offers a partial preview	• consistently uses thoughtful and insightful ideas related to the purpose • consistently employs ideas relevant to the topic • clearly offers a complete preview
Organization	• no attempt to capture the reader's attention • seldom employs a topic sentence to begin paragraphs • rarely employs effective transitions among paragraphs	• attempts interesting beginnings that hook the reader • sometimes employs a topic sentence to begin paragraphs • sometimes employs effective transitions among paragraphs	• uses interesting beginnings that hook the reader • regularly employs a topic sentence to begin paragraphs • regularly employs effective transitions among paragraphs	• uses unique beginnings that hook the reader • consistently employs a topic sentence to begin paragraphs • consistently employs effective transitions among paragraphs
Sentence Structure	• demonstrates no variety in sentence lengths • demonstrates no variety in use of sentence openers	• demonstrates little variety in sentence lengths • demonstrates little variety in use of sentence openers	• demonstrates varied sentence lengths • demonstrates varied use of sentence openers	• demonstrates effective and appropriate sentence lengths • demonstrates unique and varied use of sentence openers
Vocabulary	• chooses words that are seldom precise and unique for the audience • makes limited choices with regard to creative words	• chooses words that are sometimes precise and appropriate for the audience • begins to choose unique and creative words	• chooses words that are usually precise and appropriate for the audience • occasionally chooses unique and creative words	• chooses words that are consistently precise and appropriate for the audience • frequently chooses unique and creative words
Language Conventions	• rarely maintains appropriate tense usage • rarely uses correct punctuation • rarely uses correct spelling of high-frequency words and words important in the unit of study • rarely avoids run-on sentences	• sometimes maintains appropriate tense usage • sometimes uses correct punctuation • sometimes uses correct spelling of high-frequency words and words important in the unit of study • sometimes avoids run-on sentences	• regularly maintains appropriate tense usage • regularly uses correct punctuation • regularly uses correct spelling of high-frequency words and words important in the unit of study • regularly avoids run-on sentences	• consistently maintains appropriate tense usage • consistently uses correct punctuation • consistently uses correct spelling of high-frequency words and words important in the unit of study • consistently avoids run-on sentences

Teachers can spend many fruitless hours annotating students' compositions. Instead, Hillocks' research summary points to a productive response strategy that teachers can use to coordinate their marking of writing assignments. Besides providing feedback to students by means of rubrics, teachers offer

- a positive comment
- a suggestion based on one priority for improvement linked to a specific criterion

In some schools, teachers emphasize the value of feedback by having students keep lists of "Goals" and "Goals Achieved" (see below; a blank version of this form for classroom use appears in the Appendices at the back of this book). In primary grades, the goals form sometimes features a "Can Do" list and a "Need To Do" list.

My Writing Goals

Name: _____

Class: _____9C_____

Goals	Goals Achieved
September • vary sentences • improve clumsy sentences	October • used more complex sentences
October • use semi-colon correctly • include more detail	October • correct use of semi-colon • paragraphs more detailed
November • make introductions more interesting	November • used two different techniques to capture attention in writing tasks

Whether a school's literacy project focuses on the development of rubrics, the selection of exemplars for standard setting, or the coordination of assessment practice, literacy coaches must ensure that adequate meeting time is set aside for discussion and sharing of materials and ideas amongst team members. The rest of this chapter will explore the power of exemplar lessons that teachers can share with one another and then try out in their classrooms.

Developing Exemplar Lessons

Grade-level exemplars are necessary complements to rubrics in setting writing standards or expectations. Also, exemplars offer an equally powerful benefit as teaching tools quite apart from their standard-setting potential. Collaborative literacy projects focused on the collection of writing samples to create teaching and learning resources have become increasingly popular over the past few years.

Writing teachers recognize that rubrics "tell" about expectations and possibilities. Exemplars, on the other hand, "show" and thereby help students internalize the expectations that are listed in rubrics. Well-crafted exemplar lessons help student writers think about an author's choices.

In the following Grade 6 exemplar lesson, selected words (cued by 1a and 1b) have been omitted. Students use context to determine appropriate, evocative

Well-crafted exemplar lessons help student writers think about an author's choices.

words to fill in the blanks. Two chunks of text (marked 2a and 2b) contain simple sentences beginning with a subject. Students combine simple sentences to create complex sentences. The blank lines at the end of the story invite students to suggest an effective ending—one that offers a surprising twist, a response, or a realization.

Students do not look at the original version of the composition until they have worked with the altered version. The lesson challenges students to examine the author's choices in terms of vocabulary, sentence structure, and endings. The lesson concludes by having students revise one of their own stories to improve word choice, sentence variety, and endings. (Full-size versions of these student exemplars for classroom use appear in the Appendices at the back of this book.)

White Water Adventure
(Altered Version)

"Dad! It's too high!"

But my voice drowned in the **1a** _____ sound of the enormous rapids. Straining, I forced myself to paddle to reach my destination safely. The paddles seemed to be **1b**_____ by the power of the mighty waves.

I looked back at my dad with pleading eyes, but only saw a frustrated figure paddling vigorously, trying to steer the kayak to safety. My face was frozen with fear; I was out of control. The kayak collided with an enormous boulder, plunging my father and me into the icy, cold water. I heard the threatening roar of the waves as they rocketed against the barren cliff face. **2a** I felt myself being hurled under the powering waves. I gasped for air. My body swayed helplessly in the waves. **2b** My head crashed into a boulder. I fell unconscious.

I woke. I was in a daze. I saw a blurred figure of my father standing over me. My dad carried me to our car.

_____

_____

Grade 6 Student

White Water Adventure
(Original Version)

"Dad! It's too high!"

But my voice drowned in the thrashing sound of the enormous rapids. Straining, I forced myself to paddle to reach my destination safely. The paddles seemed to be hypnotized by the power of the mighty waves.

I looked back at my dad with pleading eyes, but only saw a frustrated figure paddling vigorously, trying to steer the kayak to safety. My face was frozen with fear; I was out of control. The kayak collided with an enormous boulder, plunging my father and me into the icy, cold water. I heard the threatening roar of the waves as they rocketed against the barren cliff face. I gasped for air. As I felt myself being hurled under the overpowering waves, my body swayed helplessly. Crashing into a boulder, I fell unconscious.

I woke. I was in a daze. I saw a blurred figure of my father standing over me. My dad carried me to our car. Groggily, I mumbled, "I told you it was too high!"

Grade 6 Student

The preceding exemplar lesson represents only one of several possible ways to use exemplars for instruction. In this case, a single writing sample challenges students to examine an author's choices. Other possibilities include:

- Presenting two versions of a sample of writing completed by the same student
- Presenting two versions of a piece of writing: the student's original version and a degraded version developed by the teacher (the teacher chooses a focus for the degraded version such as substituting a few ordinary words for colorful words)
- Presenting two versions of a piece of writing: the student's original version and an enhanced version
- Presenting two or three writing samples completed by different writers and challenging students to choose the superior sample

Exemplar lessons are most effective when students revise their own writing to enhance traits emphasized in the lesson. This pedagogy is consistent with research reported by George Hillocks in *Research on Written Composition* (1986):

> As will be seen in the meta-analysis section of this review, students who have been actively involved in the use of criteria, and/or questions to judge texts of their own or others, write compositions of significantly higher quality than those who have not. (p. 24)

> As a group these studies conclude rather clearly that engaging young writers actively in the use of criteria, applied to their own and each others' writing, results not only in more effective writing but in superior first drafts. (p. 160)

Exemplars: Your Best Resource to Improve Students' Writing (Foster and Marasco, 2007) illustrates a range of instructional possibilities for using exemplars to improve the content, organization, sentence structure, word choice, voice, and language conventions displayed in students' writing.

Collaborative projects focused on exemplars should allow time for teachers to develop exemplar lessons related to the student writing that they collect during the year. (Again, a word of caution: Teachers and literacy coaches must always respect their school jurisdiction's privacy guidelines when collecting student exemplars.) To determine the instructional impact of the exemplar lessons they develop, teachers assess the extent of beneficial revisions that they observe in their students' writing.

For example, for the "White Water Adventure" exemplar presented previously, teachers assess the number and quality of beneficial revisions in vocabulary, in sentence structure, and in the ending when students revise a piece of their own writing to conclude the lesson. One teacher observed that, following the lesson, most Grade 6 students showed improvement in their vocabulary choices and sentence structure, but only a few showed improvement in their story's ending. The teacher therefore decided that she would emphasize possibilities for strong story endings in subsequent exemplar lessons.

Throughout collaborative literacy projects focused on the creation of learning resources, literacy coaches must always ensure that adequate meeting time is set aside and that all project members have copies of the exemplar lessons—both the ones developed by the school's literacy team as well as those collected from published sources.

Checklist for Literacy Coaches and Administrators

Literacy coaches and school administrators may use this checklist to ensure they have met the following criteria in exploring and refining a collaborative literacy project related to best practice in writing instruction:

☐ We have encouraged colleagues to explore several options before choosing a focus for a collaborative writing project.

☐ We have encouraged colleagues to assess the amount of writing that students complete, including writing to learn as well as writing to communicate.

☐ We have encouraged colleagues to agree on their description of "good writing" by reviewing, selecting, and developing rubrics that demonstrate shared understanding of the characteristics of excellence in writing.

☐ We have encouraged colleagues to use group marking and the selection of exemplars to establish grade-level standards or expectations for selected writing formats.

☐ We have encouraged colleagues to assess students' ability to identify and use writing strategies before, during, and after they produce a composition.

☐ We have encouraged colleagues to assess the need to emphasize voice and other qualities that make ordinary writing extraordinary.

☐ We have encouraged colleagues to coordinate their responses to student writing.

☐ We have encouraged colleagues to develop exemplar lessons to help students improve their writing.

A Final Word

Over the past several years, I have served as a consultant on various school-based collaborative literacy projects. Many of these projects have worked extremely well; others have yielded more limited benefits to students and more limited professional satisfaction to teachers. In this book, therefore, I have advocated practices consistent with successful literacy program collaboration.

Educators vary in their level of enthusiasm for collaborative practice. However, administrators and literacy coaches can reignite confidence in colleagues who are doubtful about working together in a constructive way. Educators also vary in their ability to select a manageable common literacy goal related to the needs of their students. School leaders who can facilitate timely and focused goal setting can redirect and help sustain a project that is floundering. Educators vary in their commitment to professional development that is directly connected to their own questions, observations, and assessments. Once again, leaders—including teachers, mentors, coaches, and administrators—who are willing to promote and demonstrate the benefits of an inquiry approach to professional development can make a significant difference. Educators vary in their willingness to implement and refine instructional practice related to a collegial goal. Colleagues who show rather than simply talk about how reflective implementation of instructional practice refines practice encourage others to do the same. Educators vary in their interest in professional development that stresses creation and sharing of instructional material. Yet again, colleagues who demonstrate the benefits of the highest levels of professional development win over the skeptics.

Finally, educators vary in their enthusiasm for learning from assessment data related to collaborative literacy projects. Effective leaders exemplify how learning from assessment improves their instructional practice. Without doubt, allotting adequate time for questioning, sharing, encouraging, and celebrating fosters successful collaborative literacy projects.

My advocacy of program collaboration has been bolstered by personal observation of undeniable benefits to students. I have witnessed amazing gains in student achievement resulting from collaborative literacy instruction. Teachers are often happily surprised by the benefits revealed by documented assessment of their collaborative projects. Working together to achieve a shared vision serves students well while at the same time sustaining educators in their demanding professional roles.

Appendices

Story Bones

Story: _____

Author: _____

Main character: _____

Problem starts when _____

_____

_____

After that _____

_____

_____

Next _____

_____

_____

Then _____

_____

_____

Problem is solved when _____

_____

_____

Ending _____

_____

_____

School: _____

Timeframe for Project: _____

Participants in Project: _____

_____

Goal-Setting Activities and Dates	Goal Statement

Plan to Publicize Goal

Professional Development	Implementation Strategies	Assessment Plan
	Meeting Times _____ _____ _____ _____ _____ _____ _____ _____ _____	**Learning From Assessment**

Understanding Myself as a Reader

Name: _____ Date: _____

Title of Text: _____

Strategies I used before reading:

_____

_____

_____

_____

Strategies I used during reading:

_____

_____

_____

_____

Strategies I used after reading:

_____

_____

_____

My goals for future reading: _____

_____

_____

What I have learned about myself as a reader: _____

_____

_____

_____

Independent Reading Record

Name: _____

Title of text: _____

Author: _____

Date	Start Page	Finish Page	Pages Read	Comment, Summary, or Prediction

Narrative Elements Chart

Name: _____ Title: _____

SOMEBODY (central character)

_____

SOMEWHERE (setting)

_____

_____

WANTED (character's goal)

_____

_____

_____

BUT (conflict)

_____

_____

SO (climax)

_____

_____

_____

THEN (character's reaction)

_____

_____

_____

AND IT ALL GOES TO SHOW THAT... (theme)

_____

_____

_____

_____

Understanding Myself as a Writer

Name: _____ Date: _____

Writing assignment: _____

Strategies I used before drafting:

_____

_____

_____

_____

_____

_____

_____

_____

Strategies I used during drafting:

_____

_____

_____

_____

_____

_____

_____

_____

_____

Strategies I used after drafting:

_____

_____

_____

_____

_____

_____

_____

_____

My Writing Goals

Name: _____

Class: _____

Goals	Goals Achieved

White Water Adventure

(Altered Version)

"Dad! It's too high!"

But my voice drowned in the **1a** _____ sound of the enormous rapids. Straining, I forced myself to paddle to reach my destination safely. The paddles seemed to be **1b**_____ by the power of the mighty waves.

I looked back at my dad with pleading eyes, but only saw a frustrated figure paddling vigorously, trying to steer the kayak to safety. My face was frozen with fear; I was out of control. The kayak collided with an enormous boulder, plunging my father and me into the icy, cold water. I heard the threatening roar of the waves as they rocketed against the barren cliff face. **2a** I felt myself being hurled under the powering waves. I gasped for air. My body swayed helplessly in the waves. **2b** My head crashed into a boulder. I fell unconscious.

I woke. I was in a daze. I saw a blurred figure of my father standing over me. My dad carried me to our car. _____

_____

_____

_____

_____

Grade 6 Student

White Water Adventure

(Original Version)

"Dad! It's too high!"

But my voice drowned in the thrashing sound of the enormous rapids. Straining, I forced myself to paddle to reach my destination safely. The paddles seemed to be hypnotized by the power of the mighty waves.

I looked back at my dad with pleading eyes, but only saw a frustrated figure paddling vigorously, trying to steer the kayak to safety. My face was frozen with fear; I was out of control. The kayak collided with an enormous boulder, plunging my father and me into the icy, cold water. I heard the threatening roar of the waves as they rocketed against the barren cliff face. I gasped for air. As I felt myself being hurled under the overpowering waves, my body swayed helplessly. Crashing into a bolder, I fell unconscious.

I woke. I was in a daze. I saw a blurred figure of my father standing over me. My dad carried me to our car. Groggily, I mumbled, "I told you it was too high!"

Grade 6 Student

List of Works Consulted

Allen, Jennifer. 2006. *Becoming a Literacy Leader*. Portland, ME: Stenhouse Publishers.

Booth, David, and Jennifer Rowsell. 2007. *The Literacy Principal* (2nd Edition). Markham, ON: Pembroke Publishers.

Booth, David, and Larry Swartz. 2004. *Literacy Techniques* (2nd Edition). Markham, ON: Pembroke Publishers.

Buis, Kellie. 2007. *Reclaiming Reluctant Writers*. Markham, ON: Pembroke Publishers.

Carlson, G. Robert, and Ann Sherill. 1988. *Voices of Readers: How We Come to Love Books*. Urbana, IL: National Council of Teachers of English.

Church, Susan. 2005. *The Principal Difference*. Markham, ON: Pembroke Publishers.

Duncan, Marilyn. 2006. *Literacy Coaching*. Katonah, NY: Richard C. Owens Publishers.

Foster, Graham. 2003. *Language Arts Idea Bank*. Markham, ON: Pembroke Publishers.

Foster, Graham. 2004. *Seven Steps to Successful Writing*. Markham, ON: Pembroke Publishers.

Foster, Graham. 2005. *What Good Readers Do: Seven Steps to Better Reading*. Markham, ON: Pembroke Publishers.

Foster, Graham, and Toni L. Marasco. 2007. *Exemplars: Your Best Resource to Improve Student Writing*. Markham, ON: Pembroke Publishers.

Fullan, Michael. 2006. *Breakthrough*. Thousand Oaks, CA: Corwin Press.

Hesselbein, Frances, et al. 1999. *Leading Beyond the Walls*. Alexandria, VA: Jossey Bass.

Hillocks, George. 1986. *Research on Written Composition: New Directions for Teaching*. Urbana, IL: National Council of Teachers of English.

Hillocks, George. 1995. *Teaching Writing as Reflective Practice*. New York, NY: Teachers College Press.

Hinson, Bess (ed.) 2000. *New Directions in Reading Instruction* (Revised). Newark, DL: International Reading Association.

Lieberman, Ann, and Lynne Miller. 2000. *Teacher Leadership*. San Francisco, CA: John Wiley & Sons.

Loucks-Horsely, Susan, et al. 1996. "Professional Development for Science Education: A Critical and Immediate Challenge." National Standards and the Science Curriculum. Dubuque, IO: Kendall Hunt.

Marzano, Robert J., et al. 2005. *School Leadership That Works*. AlexandrIa, VA: Association for Supervision and Curriculum Development.

Moffett, James. 1968. *Teaching: The Universe of Discourse*. New York, NY: Houghton Mifflin.

Parsons, Les. 2001. *Response Journals Revisited*. Markham, ON: Pembroke Publishers.

Senge, Peter M. 2006. *The Fifth Discipline: The Art and Practice of the Learning Organization*. New York, NY: Doubleday.

Serafini, Frank. 2004. *Lessons in Comprehension: Explicit Instruction in the Reading Workshop*. Portsmouth, NH: Heinemann.

Sweeney, Diane. 2003. *Learning Along the Way: Professional Development by and for Teachers*. Portland, ME: Stenhouse Publishers.

Taylor, Rosmarye, and Valerie Doyle Collins. 2003. *Literacy Leadership for Grades 5-12*. Alexandria, VA: Association for Supervision and Curriculum Development.

Tomlinson, Carol Ann. 1999. *The Differentiated Classroom: Responding to the Needs of All Learners*. Alexandria, VA: Association for Supervision and Curriculum Development.

Wild, Monique D., Amanda S. Mayeux, and Kathryn P. Edmonds. 2008. *Teamwork: Setting the Standard for Collaborative Teaching, Grades 5–9*. Portland, ME: Stenhouse Publishers; Westerville, OH: National Middle School Association.

Index

Acknowledgments

The author gratefully acknowledges the advice of Dr. Jean Hoeft, Calgary Regional Professional Development Consortium; Wes Oginski, Rockyview School Division; and Dr. Lynne Paradis, Red Deer Catholic School District. In addition, the author acknowledges the educators and students of Banff Elementary School in Banff, Alberta. Their collaboration with the author on a two-year writing strategies project confirmed the program coordination model advocated in this book. Thanks to Steve Greene, Deb Cavanaugh, Kathryn Walton, Genia Luchka, Valerie Heath, Maxine Achurch, Connie Beatson, Jennifer Delay, Barb Skinner, Nicole Ryan, Marilyn Kimmitt, Bronwyn Richards, Sue Moleski, Carl Shields, Chantal Leclerc, Mary Paston, Susan George, Ginette Hulsmans, Margaret Feist, Shannon Perron, Barb Sarna, Pam Barrett, Janis Bekar, Terri Williamson, Louise Bianchi, Anita Becker, Allyson Van Impe, Amy Heath, Jessica Schovanek, Mary Buckingham, and Donna McCuaig.